PRAISE FOR A SUMMER STORY
OF GOD'S ENDURING GRACE

Against a bedrock of tenacious faith, LaQuita Propes revisits her family's season of heartbreak. With eloquent honesty, she leads us down their path of adversity and pain. With extraordinary insight, she challenges us to take advantage of our intervals, to embrace our interruptions. With quiet resolve, she reminds us that the seasons of our lives will change, but the Author and Finisher of our faith never will.

This is a story of intervals, of interruptions, of seasonal transitions. It is a bird's-eye view of a family forced to navigate the periphery of uncertainty as they journey through the valley of the shadow.

—Janet Paschal

Gospel Singer/Author

Much like most everyone's favorite season of the year, her very name evokes warmth and sunshine. Her personality, tender heart, and glowing demeanor radiates the love of Jesus to all who meet her. But her promising season known as *life* was almost cut extremely short in a most challenging and heartbreaking way. Many have often stated the euphemism, "What a difference a day makes." But in Summer's case, it should have been rephrased to say, "What a difference a minute makes."

One minute, everything seemed so right. The next, it seemed that only death itself could make things worse. Summer has had too many of those minutes. Yet, over and over again, God stepped in and out of eternity to make time work for and not against her. As a result, hundreds have been touched by her story, encouraged by her resolve, and inspired by her faith. The book you are about to read is not a second-hand story heard and retold from a distance, but, rather, one that was lived out minute-by-every-excruciating-yet-miraculous minute as a result of a faithful mother and praying father.

Summer's story will melt the coldest hearts and bring the brightness of sunlight to the darkest circumstances. Read it and allow trust to be rekindled in your heart.

—Dr. Tim Hill

General Director

Church of God World Missions, Cleveland, Tennessee

The greatest pain for a mother is not childbirth but watching her offspring suffer. LaQuita Propes has experienced this darkness of ministering to her daughter during unimaginable physical and emotional trauma. She continues to care for Summer's special needs with great grace and formidable faith.

A Summer Story will inspire you to trust the Lord in the face of impossible circumstances and even give thanks for those challenges and struggles.

—Sandra Kay Williams
International Women's Director
Church of God, Cleveland, Tennessee

So many things come to mind as I recall the occurrences LaQuita Propes shares in *A Summer Story*. The first thought is of Summer herself and of her loving personality. There has always been a certain temperament about her that softly declares, "I am exceptional." My wife, Vickie, and I have never been around her when we didn't get the feeling that she radiated genuine affection and the sparkle of a warm *summer* day with the comfort of a warm *summer* breeze. Through all of her suffering, Summer Propes has brought peace and joy to so many.

Then, too, I think of the tender love and dedication of a mother, father, and brother who have embraced Summer with an uncommon devotion and resplendent love. *A Summer Story* is an incredible read, and is certain to help individuals cope with life when things don't go as planned. LaQuita Propes provides us with an incredible example of how to trust God when human answers simply aren't enough.

—Dr. R. Lamar Vest
Former General Overseer of the Church of God
President Emeritus of American Bible Society

A Summer Story is a remarkably written book in which each word touches the heart and soul of the reader. It is certainly a faith-building book, which reminds all of us that as a child of God, everything is sifted through His loving hands. The book proves once again that in the midst of our storms, God is holding us and giving us strength to persevere. All we have to do is call on Him and have faith.

This book is definitely a "must read" for the believer, as it is one of the most spiritually uplifting books I have read. For unbelievers, it is a true account of God at work. After reading it, I now look to God and at life with a deeper and a more positive perspective, and one thing is clear: Life should be a dance with God, and He should lead.

This is a wonderful narrative of God's handiwork—past, present, and into the future. You will be blessed and will desire a closer walk with the Lord Jesus when you read *A Summer Story* . . . and you will keep the book handy for a reminder of His faithfulness.

—Marian Johnson

Executive Director, Florida Chamber Political Institute

For a number of years, the Propes family has been dear friends. Even with this close friendship and being fully aware of the crisis this precious family faced, I never really understood the depth of it all until I read *A Summer*

Story. This book describes how a family faced one of life's toughest challenges and how they were able to cope with it—especially the mother who felt that special point of pain when her child was suffering so much. While reading, I witnessed so much faith and felt the power of that faith flowing through her story that I walked away from it feeling a renewed element of faith I had not felt in some time.

LaQuita Propes' book about her sweet daughter, Summer, her near-death experience and constant challenges, coupled with the revealing stories of their faith under fire, will lift your soul and encourage your heart. I heartily endorse it and trust you will too!

—Donnie W. Smith, D.Min.
Executive Administrator, Division of Care
Church of God, Cleveland, Tennessee

Every song, every story, every miracle in this book recounts the glorious grace of God's work in Summer Propes' life. From the countless prayers, to the committed family and friends, to the constant source of strength expressed through hugs and hallelujahs, each remarkable memory becomes a stone. Each miracle becomes a memorial—a memorial from God.

When you close the last chapter of *A Summer Story,* you will realize that each incident is a miracle that all started on a Memorial Day weekend. As you read these incredible chapters, you will cry, you will laugh, you will sing, you may even dance. And, as the last chapter encourages, I hope you dance!

—Kevin D. Brooks, Representative
Tennessee 24th District
Public Relations and Conference Manager
Church of God, Cleveland, Tennessee

A Summer Story

...OF GOD'S ENDURING GRACE

LaQuita Propes

with

Wanda Griffith

Pathway Press

Book Editor: Lance Colkmire
Editorial Assistant: Tammy Hatfield
Copy Editor: Esther Metaxas
Inside Layout: Gale Ard
Cover Design: Michael McDonald
Cover Photos by Tracie Birch (*lifeprintsbytracie.com*)

ISBN: 978-1-59684-796-5

DEDICATION

To my husband of thirty-seven years, M. Thomas
(Tommy to me),
who has been my love through it all.
He is the only one who truly knows what this journey
has been. I would not want to do this without him.
He has my heart.

To Matthew and Jennifer,
the best son and "daughter-in-love"
anyone could ever ask for.
They give unselfishly and are so understanding.
They bring us much happiness;
and
Summer, this is your story. I love you, sweet girl.

CONTENTS

ACKNOWLEDGMENTS

I am forever grateful . . .

To my parents, who raised me to love God and love others.

To family and friends who have loved us, encouraged us, and remained with us.

To the places we have been blessed to serve before Summer's journey of suffering began: Live Oak Church of God, Hinesville, Georgia; Jesup Church of God, Jesup, Georgia; and the Church of God in the Great Lakes Region. You loved us and taught us much. And then afterward: Church of God in Northern Ohio; Pathway Press, Cleveland, Tennessee; and Church of God in South Carolina. What would we have done without you all! I am so thankful God knows where to place you for such a time as this.

To the staff and doctors at Children's Hospital in Akron, Ohio; T.C. Thompson Children's Hospital in Chattanooga, Tennessee; Egleston Children's Hospital and Emory University Hospital in Atlanta, Georgia—which have all been wonderful. I believe they all did their best. I'm thankful for their knowledge and loving care for Summer.

To everyone who has "shared a driveway" with us. We have felt your love, your prayers, and your patience.

To Dr. Bill George for giving advice when this project was being birthed. He remains a faithful friend.

To Pathway Press—Terry Hart, general director, and Raymond Hodge, administrative assistant—for their confidence in this project. Also, to Ora Hart, marketing and public relations facilitator for keeping this project on task.

To my husband's executive assistants—Belinda Sherlin and Denise Watkins—for their support and encouragement.

To my dear friend, Wanda Griffith. I have known her a long time but became more acquainted with her when my husband was general director of publications at Pathway Press. We have attended a few events together and shared some good times. I never expected to work with her in this capacity, but I'm so grateful for her expertise. This project would not be fulfilled without her.

Most of all, to my heavenly Father, whose enduring grace keeps my days secure.

FOREWORD

As a mother of three, I can't imagine the anguish parents must feel having to watch their own child suffer. It has to be one of the most grueling experiences in life. Our hearts break just to see a child suffer with a fever, but to endure an ongoing battle with seizures and brain surgeries must be more than a parent can bear.

Yet, in *A Summer Story*, my dear friend LaQuita Propes paints a complex portrait of the unfailing love of a parent, the uplifting moments of a faithful God and faithful friends, and the strength found when facing heartbreak during difficult times.

Bringing readers into her life of constant care for her special-needs daughter, she captivates us with humor and the triumphant moments of a young woman with a child's mind.

A Summer Story is a tender and, at times, funny picture of the lives of a family with a special-needs child, the enduring care that requires patience and a consistent schedule, and the aid of friends and family who come alongside to assist. All of these factors make for a book that will bring tears and applause to the Propes family for their tenacity and constant faith in a loving Father God who cares for them.

Encouraging and inspiring, this is one book that will remind you that we serve a faithful God who remains constant even in the face of difficult circumstances of life.

–Joni Lamb, Cofounder
Daystar Television Network

SUMMER JOY

When I was a young girl, I always watched the

televised beauty pageants.

One year, a beautiful girl named *Summer*

won the crown, and I thought,

If I ever have a little girl, I will call her Summer.

Thankfully, years later after I was married

and had a baby girl,

my husband liked the name, too.

I even got to give her my middle name . . .

and a *Summer Joy* was born.

INTRODUCTION

Life is not a journey you want to make on "autopilot," because things can change in a moment. My beautiful daughter, Summer Joy, was born March 2, 1989. She had no major problems except for a two- to three-year developmental delay. She was learning, thriving in school, and taking no medications. Just like her name, she was full of sunshine and joy.

Then on May 25, 2002, our lives changed forever. This Saturday was filled with the typical things—shopping, eating out, doing laundry, planting flowers outside, having dinner, and then preparing for church the next morning. During Summer's bath that evening, I ran downstairs to change the clothes from the washer to the dryer. As I passed the bottom of the stairs, I heard a dreadful cry that said to me, *Summer is in pain; something terrible has happened!* Mothers have that sixth sense that can distinguish the difference in certain cries, and this was one I had never heard before.

A SUMMER STORY
OF GOD'S ENDURING GRACE

As I rushed upstairs to see what was happening, my heart was a bundle of fear and horror. The small stuff of life became insignificant, and the long nightmare of 911 calls, hospital visits, brain surgeries, and diminishing health began. My baby was crying with a headache. Her eye and the left side of her head looked red, but I thought it was from her pressing on it.

My heart was heavy—struck with panic and confusion about the situation. As I helped her out of the tub, she wouldn't even let me dry her off. She ran and fell on the bed, screaming with pain. My first thought was to grab the bottle of Tylenol for her. When I got back to her room, she was standing at the television, trying to turn it off. With an earsplitting shout, she held her head and cried, "It's too loud! It's too loud!" She always used the remote, so I knew something was especially strange.

As I gave her the medicine, I noticed that when she looked at me, she was not focusing on my face; I knew something was terribly wrong. My husband heard the crying and came to see what was happening. Still crying, Summer told him her head hurt, and immediately she seemed to fall asleep. At first I thought she was just exhausted from crying, but then I realized she was unconscious.

What followed was a time of horrifying silence. Summer didn't say another word or make another sound until after seven hours of brain surgery six days later. I lived in the waiting room and didn't leave the hospital for the next thirteen days, except to run home and pay bills. During those long days, Dr. Mike Baker, director of Church of God Communications, sent out the first of two *Alert mails* to church leaders asking for special prayer. We received calls from all over the world reassuring us that people were praying for us. I drew a map of the United States and, as calls were received, I colored the area representing the state being covered in prayer. Calls came from Germany, Austria, Canada, and all fifty states! How many times we thought, *How great it is to have such a wonderful church family.*

Nothing about this journey of pain makes any sense if we are only spectators sitting in the stands. God invites His children to meet Him on the "field" of suffering. This is where we risk everything to know His heart and His will right now in our desperate situation. How He enters that game is the best adventure novel you will ever read—only it's your own life and you are actually living it! The only thing He asks is that you cling to Him and resist the urge to crawl back into the stands.

The underlying premise of this book is that we stay on the field, taking each step of faith with a relentless trust in His Word that promises: "Do not be afraid or terrified . . . for the Lord your God goes with you; he will never leave you nor forsake you" (Deut. 31:6).

A SUMMER STORY
OF GOD'S ENDURING GRACE

What a message of hope—hope that is pinned to God and His goodness, rather than to people. This hope has a buoyancy that is grounded, not in our own illusion of how our story should read, but in the character of God. As David wrote in the Psalms:

> I would have despaired unless I had believed that
>
> I would see the goodness of the Lord
>
> In the land of the living.
>
> Wait for the Lord;
>
> Be strong and let your heart take courage;
>
> Yes, wait for the Lord (27:13-14 NASB).

He asks His children to walk with Him through the blood and guts of their real experience in an honest pilgrimage where they let Him show them what real strength is all about. This book will be a guide to helping the reader submit earthly ties and say yes to the call to become a stronger, wiser, and loving person God created. Along the way, each traveler will encounter the fear of facing the future and the need to trust Him more fully—important subjects for any who would travel well.

CHAPTER ONE

Testing comes into our lives to make us more flexible, to move us out of our comfort zones.

—Mike Breen and Walt Kallestad

FIGHTING FOR HER LIFE

MEMORIAL DAY WEEKEND IS A TIME I WILL NEVER forget. Outside, a storm was brewing and the wind was howling with a terrific force. While taking her bath, Summer screamed with pain in her head. We immediately called 911. I had to dress her limp body while she was still unconscious. Before long, seven paramedics were at our house, working feverously on her before transporting her to Children's Hospital in Akron, Ohio.

As we hurried out the door, I remember thinking, *Summer would surely catch pneumonia because her hair is still wet.* I rode in the front of the ambulance and my husband followed in the car. We were both praying for our precious daughter, who was fighting for her life.

On the way to the hospital, Tommy called the state evangelism director, Thomas Gillum, and asked him and his family to pray. Looking in the back of the ambulance, I watched as her body posture would stiffen and suspend off the bed. Then she would remain still for a few moments, and then repeat the motion. She had rapidly gone into a critical state, and her body was seizing.

Miracles Along the Way

God is always at work around us. Our evangelism director's son-in-law, Kevin Henry, was a doctor in residency and his schedule allowed him to be at Children's Hospital occasionally. It was a blessing to see him when we arrived at the hospital, since he was usually at City Hospital. His presence was such a comfort for us. When he heard the ambulance call that a special-needs thirteen-year-old was being transported to the hospital, he thought of Summer, not knowing it was actually her. We were so grateful he was on duty.

Kevin and his wife, Christa, had stayed with Summer several times while we were away on business, so they knew her and loved her. To have him attending Summer was like having family in the ER with her when we couldn't be there. I could look through the door and see him rubbing her foot and, no doubt, praying for her. Then he would come out occasionally and keep us informed of what was happening while we waited outside.

We learned that our neurosurgeon hadn't been at Children's Hospital for very long, but he had a great reputation. We were so thankful he was there. His bedside manner would not get him voted into "Most Likeable" category, but maybe we were looking for more than he could give us. We wanted to connect with him, but how to accomplish this, we weren't sure. Then we discovered that his daughter was in Christa's class at Lady of the Elms. Now out of the 250,000 people in Akron, what are the chances that this would happen? This was just another miracle we saw God do along the way.

Recently, I was able to talk to Dr. Henry, who shared with me some of his thoughts:

"I remember seeing Brother Propes down the hallway and wondering what was going on. I certainly had concern, but as I made my way into the exam room and saw Summer, my concern turned to fear. When you see somebody you know in that situation, you know she is in good hands with the staff that was there that night, so I wasn't worried about that. But having somebody you know and care about in that situation that turned out to be life-threatening is very disconcerting. And then the overwhelming thought of, *Oh, goodness, what is going on?* I was trying to help you all through that, give you some answers, and see what I could do to help."

In the exam room, he said, "There was much concern with her condition because she was already having the seizures even before we had the diagnosis. When she arrived, she was in pretty rough shape, so I didn't know for sure what was going on. We had to get to the CT scan first. Looking into the control room and seeing the bleed, I'm wondering, *Is it from a tumor or from an aneurysm? What is causing this?* Right away you don't know for sure. Then we had to put her on the ventilator. All those things certainly were not pleasant."

For Kevin to be there on that particular day and that particular shift was amazing. He said, "It was an ordained thing." He was not scheduled there again during Summer's stay, but he came back to visit and check on her while she was in ICU.

Kevin and Christa now live in the Chattanooga, Tennessee, area and he works at Memorial Hospital. I'm so glad we are close again. I hope we don't ever need him, but if we do, I hope he's on duty.

As a Christian, a great deal of abiding in Christ is asking and waiting. I confess that I don't do either very well. I think that's because both asking and especially the waiting requires that I acknowledge I am not in control. That's when I rely on His Word that assures me: "He gives strength to the weary and increases the power of the weak" (Isa. 40:29).

"Round One" of Her Fight

The first CT scan revealed that Summer had suffered a near-fatal cerebral hemorrhage. Her left temporal lobe had burst. It appeared that the bleeding had stopped at the present time, so she was stabilized and placed in a medically induced coma. We really wouldn't know anymore until further tests were conducted, and they wanted to wait until after the holiday weekend to schedule an angiogram. The test was scheduled for Tuesday after Memorial Day. We had to endure more anxious hours of waiting and praying.

I refused to leave the hospital, so Cathy Gillum brought me some of her clothes to wear. I loved wearing them because it was like having a new wardrobe. My friends thought of every tiny detail—even thinking about our son, Matthew, so he wouldn't be at home by himself. Others were there for us, including Barbara and O. L. Henderson, my husband's assistant, and our local pastor, Rick and Doris Fuson. The next day my parents arrived from

Georgia, as well as the state youth director, Chuck and Sharon Noel, who had been traveling. What a source of comfort they all were to us. Over the next several days, there was a steady stream of people who came to the hospital.

I found a handicapped-accessible bathroom stall on the floor where we were waiting that became my prayer closet. It was large enough so that I could pace back and forth and call on His precious name.

More Complications

While in the hospital, Summer started running a fever, and they placed her on a cooling blanket. She looked so peaceful. They had bandaged her head completely and didn't want us to talk to her for fear of her hearing our voice and getting upset. They wanted her to be completely still. She also developed a pressure sore on her tailbone in ICU and had severe complications from that. This was more painful, along with diarrhea, than other things.

There is no rest in the hospital. Therapists came in at all hours of the day, asking me questions. This was somewhat annoying because the questions seemed frivolous, but I'm sure they were just doing their job. Summer was grumpy and didn't want any part of it. I tried to be nice, but I didn't want them upsetting her. They had to put braces on her legs so her muscles would not atrophy. The braces were quite uncomfortable and she didn't like them at all.

During this time, the words to one of my favorite songs by Janet Paschal became a comfort to me:

God Will Make a Way

Must have felt strange to end up stranded between
an army and the sea.
They must have felt forsaken, wondering
why God wasn't all He said He'd be.
When your back's against the wall,
it's the hardest place of all.
But somewhere between provisions and impossibility . . .

God will make a way
when there seems to be no way.
Forever He is faithful.
He will make a road
when you bear a heavy load.
I know, God will make a way.

When a wall of circumstances leaves
you crying in the night,
And you struggle till your strength is almost gone,
God will gently hold you in the shelter of His heart
And carve a road for you to carry on.
So carry on.

Words and Music by Janet Paschal
Maplesong Music/ASCAP, BMG Music/BMI@1997

We would certainly carry on with this fight. With so many family members and friends praying for us and encouraging us, we would not be "knocked out."

Words of Hope

Eleanor Sheeks gave me the scripture in 1 Peter 3:12: "The eyes of the Lord watch over those who do right, and his ears are open to their prayers" (NLT). Throughout the times of waiting, we held on to those words of hope, knowing our church touched God for the healing of our little girl. We heard reports of similar cases where the same thing happened to a thirteen-year-old and an eighteen-year-old who did not survive. I don't know *why* God spared Summer's life, but He had a purpose. He knows the future because He is already there.

It had been a long process, but the fight would continue. We would hold to God's unchanging hand and prepare for "round two"!

The following message was given to me prophetically six days before our journey with Summer's hemorrhagic stroke.

Evangelist Phyllis Alexander (May 19, 2002) at the East Market Street Church of God Revival:

*You will shift from where you are to your next level, and I break
the weight in Jesus' name. The Lord says, "Always giving out."
He says, "Always giving out, always giving out." He says, "This
night He places within you that which is needed for this next
level that you've been shifted to."*

Little did I know what the next level would be. Then
one year exactly to the date as the previous message, I received another word from the Lord.

Dr. Elizabeth Sikes (May 19, 2003) at Sandy Valley
Church of God:

*There has been a period of time of difficulty in your family, but
God has a limitation on it. When you don't know what to do,
"Ask Me," the Lord says. The healing has begun layer by layer,
step by step. This is in God's plan. She will touch more lives
than you can ever imagine, and she has already touched lives.
God says, "Your pure faith in Me that you never question; I
am going to honor it." The ministry will go on to both of your
children, not just one, but both.*

We don't know the cost of another person's praise. I
wish I didn't have this story to tell. I wish I could have had
the normal life of seeing my beautiful daughter turn into
a special woman doing all the girly things, from proms to
weddings to having children, but God had a different plan.
I'm thankful all the same, even though it's different than I
expected. At least I didn't have to bury my child.

A SUMMER STORY
OF GOD'S ENDURING GRACE

During the many times my husband and I have shared snippets of Summer's story, people have always come up to us and wanted to know more of her story, or saying, "We are going through the same thing; would you pray for us?"

We have also had people share with us their personal experiences of a brain hemorrhage that have been so helpful to us, because we had no idea of the pain Summer felt. But they will tell us, "That was the most severe headache ever; like a thunderclap. I have not experienced pain like that since."

God has placed many special people in our lives—some for a lifetime, others for a season—but all are appreciated. I'm so thankful for God's presence. It is my desire that all who read her story will be given hope for their situation. It is difficult to relive all the painful experiences, but I don't want to miss the opportunity that God could use them to encourage or strengthen someone. I heard someone say, "Turn your mess into a message." I guess that is what I'm doing.

DR. HENRY, SUMMER, AND CHRISTA
IN THE HOSPITAL HAVING HER FIRST BABY

CHAPTER TWO

You must do the thing which you think you cannot do.

—Eleanor Roosevelt

THE SURGERY

During this process of waiting for results from medical tests, I learned that the pathway to healing is often paved with knee-prints. The angiogram showed the 6-centimeter bleed in Summer's brain, which meant surgery would be needed to repair a condition called *arteriovenous malformation*, an abnormal connection of blood vessels. We were told that this is the leading cause of strokes in young children. I couldn't wrap my brain around it—Summer had suffered a stroke. Unbelievable!

The surgery would take about seven hours, and her neurological state could not be determined until afterward. The hemorrhage was in the most critical area on the left side of her brain, which controls the right side of her body, her motor skills, her speech, and the ability to process things.

The writer of Hebrews says:

The word of God is living and active. Sharper than any double-edged sword, it penetrates even to dividing soul and spirit, joints and marrow; it judges the thoughts and attitudes of the heart (4:12).

The kind of procedure described here is *surgery*. Anyone who has ever had surgery knows that whether it is physical or spiritual, surgery is both frightening and painful—especially for a young child.

A Place of Grace

The neurosurgeon in charge of Summer told us, "After surgery, she may understand what you're saying, but she won't be able to respond; or she may not have a clue of what you are saying." But we knew and trusted the Master Surgeon. He was in control of the situation, even when the days grew dark and words were not strong enough to make everything right; we had a place of shelter, healing, and grace.

The surgery was scheduled for Wednesday, May 29, 2002, and we knew God would guide the hands of the surgeon. Summer remained stable throughout the surgery. Her body temperature remained normal, and she didn't require any blood transfusions. After what seemed to be an eternity, the seven-hour surgery was complete and the situation looked hopeful.

During the last days in intensive care, Summer would cry out through her oxygen mask, "Oh, my God. Help me, Jesus!" She would say it so loud and with an attitude that I would try to quiet her so she wouldn't disturb other patients. But someone nearby said, "It's OK . . . I know she is going to be all right because she is calling on the right Person."

A "Ray" of Hope

They said it would be at least twenty-four hours before she would be taken off the ventilator, but in less time than that, the machines were removed and she was taken off of life support. Shortly afterward, her bandage was removed, and she was recognizing family and friends. Even though she had been in the coma when my parents were there, when she awakened, she asked for Papa, knowing he had been there earlier.

She looked so pitiful. Her head was swollen, her left eye was swollen shut, and her head was shaved on one side, but she was calling everyone by name. What a welcome sign to know that she recognized us. One of the greatest signs of recovery was that she remembered vividly what had happened prior to her going into unconsciousness in her bedroom.

Our Private Room

Days transpired before she was able to move her right side, but as prayers continued, the miracle continued. After nine days in intensive care, we were able to move her into a private room . . . and were we ever thankful! At last I could abandon the knotty couch I had been sleeping on in the waiting room and the chair by her bed. And most of all, no longer would I have to take showers on the seventh floor (even though that was a great shower), and no more swollen ankles from sitting and sleeping in a chair. Now we had our very own room, full of stuffed animals and flowers. Best of all, we had a bathroom and couch that made into a bed. Shortly afterward, Doris Fuson delivered the best Italian meal ever. The world seemed almost normal again. I didn't realize, then, that life would never be the same. Daily, sometimes hourly, we asked the doctors, "When can we go home?"

The Dream

On Saturday night, May 25, 2002, Bonnie Tompkins had a dream about Summer. She was in a room that appeared to be a hospital room, lying in a bed with her eyes closed, unable to wake up. In the dream, Bonnie sensed there was a crisis, but she didn't understand what was happening. Wanting to comfort Summer, she lifted her upon her shoulder and began rubbing her head, praying for the pain to stop. Placing her back down on the pillow, Bonnie kissed Summer on the forehead and whispered that she was going to be all right; she would be going home in a few days.

Bonnie then described the calm peace that assured her Summer was going to be all right. The next scene in the dream was Tommy with Summer in his arms, placing her in the car to go home. As I turned to get in the car, I asked Bonnie, "Is Homer [Bonnie's husband] going to church?"

"No, but I still believe he will."

"I promise you, he will," I said as I hugged Bonnie.

When Bonnie woke up, she was crying and told Homer, "You will never guess who I dreamed about last night."

Immediately he said, "Tommy Propes."

"Why did you say that?" Bonnie asked.

"Because I was in the dream."

"Yes you were . . . in a way," Bonnie said, describing the dream to her husband. Then he insisted that she call and find out what was going on. Making excuses—such as she didn't have the number, what would she say, and maybe we would think she was crazy—Bonnie went on to church with a heavy heart. Pastor Poole and a friend were in the office, so Bonnie shared the dream and asked them to pray for her.

Later while speaking at a ladies meeting, Debby Davis came in and said, "I hate to interrupt the meeting, but we need to pray right now. Summer Propes had a brain hemorrhage and is in critical condition."

As Bonnie looked at her friend (who knew about her dream), she said her legs felt like jelly. Pastor Poole called the entire church to prayer for Summer. When Bonnie got home, Homer said she should call us and tell us about her dream on Saturday night. Tommy answered the phone and said the doctors were not giving the family much hope. "Can you tell me anything to give me hope?" he asked.

Bonnie described the end of the dream when she saw Summer in her daddy's arms, going home from the hospital. "The devil played mind games with me, telling me Summer was going to die and I was going to look like a fool," Bonnie explained, "but I kept believing that what I saw in the dream would come true—and it did!"

Home at Last

Loading two SUVs with flowers and gifts, we headed for home, so excited to be on our way. Little did we know how we would miss the hospital staff's expertise! We still had so many questions in this unknown territory of medical care. Summer weighed only sixty-three pounds, could not even walk alone, and she needed assistance for everything, but we leaned heavily on God's Word. Psalm 41:1-2 became our prayer:

> Blessed is he who has regard for the weak; the Lord delivers him in times of trouble.
> The Lord will protect him and preserve his life.

We were desperate, living in that weak but preservation stage, thanking God every day for each tiny ray of hope. It is only in our rest and in His refuge that we become wooed by our Redeemer. He makes our hearts tender when we take time to "marinate" in His love and mercy.

The next phase would be occupational, speech, and physical therapy. We just thought if we could get home we would all be together again as a family. We promised we would bring her back for those appointments. The date was June 6; we were going home, and we were so thankful, but there were more "mountains" to climb!

Three times a week for eight weeks, we took Summer for therapy. Those trips were grueling, but we kept our promise. We were serving Northern Ohio as the state overseer, and our camp meeting was sandwiched in there somewhere; but with the help from the most wonderful staff, we made it through. Then, fifteen months later, another battle began; she started having seizures.

Seizures

In August 2003, Summer and I were having a typical day at home. I had just prepared her lunch, and she was eating from her tray while watching a DVD. Tommy was out of town preaching in Pennsylvania.

All of a sudden I heard her scream, "Help me . . . help me . . . help me!" After her surgery, when she would get upset, she had become a little more demanding in her tone. When you add in the drama of a teenage girl, well, you can have somewhat of a diva! I guess God knew she would have to be tough to make it through.

I ran in there to see her tray knocked over and she was in a full-body convulsion. I had never seen anyone have a seizure, so I wasn't sure this was what it was. I immediately dialed 911 and told them, "Please hurry; something has happened to my daughter, and I think she may be having a seizure!"

I knelt down beside her and was screaming, "Oh, honey, what's wrong . . . what's wrong?" In between that, I was praying loudly and asking God for mercy. I thought the ambulance should have already been there, so I called again. They assured me they were on their way. There was road construction and they had to take an alternate route. I begged them, "Please hurry!"

Later I found out she could hear what I was saying when all of this was going on, because she said, "Why were you screaming and asking me what was wrong? I tried to tell you!"

I never screamed in her ear again.

Upon arriving, the EMTs assessed her, and immediately transported her to the hospital. Again, I rode in the ambulance. This time, I had a cell phone because I remember trying to call my husband and some others, but to no avail. I finally reached Tommy and he immediately was en route home. I am sure that was a long drive—longer than usual—and I believed he called everyone he could think of. Shortly after, the state youth director, Chuck and Sharon Noel, arrived. They had been at a family reunion and didn't have cell service. Others from the state office and our local church where we attended also arrived.

The doctor decided to keep us overnight and scheduled her for an EEG in about three weeks. She was still not placed on a medication because they said sometimes it happens only once, and they needed to see if that was the case. Sadly, it wasn't the case.

Over the next few weeks as we were waiting for the EEG, we noticed some "episodes" to the tune of about thirteen in nine days. The EEG came back abnormal, so the neurologist prescribed the first of many anti-seizure drugs. The episodes immediately lessened to about three in eight days.

So, Summer had experienced her first generalized seizure (grand mal). The timing of this was a miracle within itself, because she was supposed to have stayed with my parents while we were enrolling Matthew in Lee University, but plans changed and she didn't. The reason this is such a miracle is that my parents lived on Lake Seminole in the tristate area of southwest Georgia. The best hospital that could have handled this type of emergency would have been either Dothan, Alabama, or Tallahassee, Florida. I don't even think EMT services were available, so they would have had to make the drive of about forty-five minutes either way. As God would have it, we had made it home to Ohio and back to Children's Hospital in Akron.

THE SURGERY

More Seizures

Then the wild ride begins with more seizures, different medications, and dealing with the side effects. This is a continuous battle. Sometimes I wonder which is worse: the seizures or the meds. Particular medicines are miracles for some individuals but nightmares for others. It is trial and error, and it is not pleasant. Reading the side effects that are three inches long on written paper makes you physically sick to your stomach to have to give the medicine to your child, but then it only takes one generalized seizure to understand and make the decision. We worry about her internal organs. There are always many blood tests to make sure things are OK. The doctors tell us if it shows up on the blood work, it is probably too late. So why do we do the tests? I don't know.

The type of seizures that are specific to Summer are *partial* and *generalized*. The partials can either be simple or complex, and one presents itself with a series of loud screams, followed by panic, rapid pulse, loss of coordination, and right-side body contractions. She usually has an aura, and the postictal period can last up to one hour.

The other type starts with some type of moaning and tremors. She fidgets back and forth, then she will go into a trancelike state for a few minutes. She drools, contracts, and is nonresponsive. She can have loss of bladder control. Then she will cough and start to recover. She has no recollection of this type. I'm not really sure which one is which, but we handle them the same—attend to her, making sure her airway is open, and assuring her that all is well.

The generalized—or *grand mals*, as they were called in earlier days—usually transitions from a partial seizure. She has total loss of body control with full-body convulsions, is nonresponsive, and has a lot of facial twitching. Normally, she starts pointing to her right eye, meaning she sees a light. This type of seizure will cause Summer to go into *status epilepticus*, which is a medical emergency. At first we had to call the EMTs every time, but then they gave us *Diastat*, which we administer quickly via a rectal gel injection. Thankfully, we only have about two per year. Anytime you see Summer, you know Diastat is with her.

Seizures cause a lot of anxiety, panic, fear, and stress for her. Her face loses complete color and turns gray. Her hands and feet perspire, and she feels a burning sensation (like a fire) in her stomach. Her mouth can also draw up at the corner. It is devastating to see your child go through something like this. She can have about eighteen to twenty-two seizures per month, even with the handful of medications she takes. I have to keep a separate calendar with the seizure activity noted. We are always on "seizure alert."

On Thanksgiving night a couple of years ago, while returning home to Greenville from a family reunion, Summer suffered not one . . . but five generalized seizures. Never has this happened! We used the emergency meds we carry with us, all to no avail. With no other options, we called EMS and they met us in Madison, Georgia (one of the smallest towns we travel through!).

They took her to the hospital to stabilize her and then discussed transporting her to Emory (in Atlanta), where her doctor is. Thankfully, after instructions from Emory, we were able to go home and schedule an appointment after the holiday. This was just too much excitement for this stage of my life (some of you understand).

During all of life's difficulties—especially during holidays—know that I understand if your life isn't perfect. I'm praying for you, and together with God's grace, we will make it.

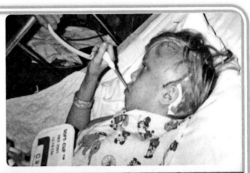

BRAIN
HEMORRHAGE/
STROKE
EMERGENCY
SURGERY 2002

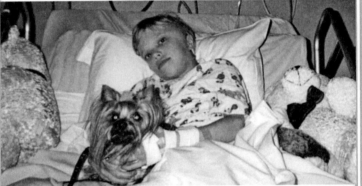

VICKIE VEST, DR. R. LAMAR VEST, SUMMER AND BETHANY
NORTHERN OHIO CAMP MEETING
TWO WEEKS FOLLOWING THE STROKE

CHAPTER THREE

*Seasons of dryness prepare us
for the flood.*

MAJOR CHALLENGES

THROUGH THE MANY CHALLENGES WE HAVE FACED, I'VE learned that life is not a trial run . . . it's the only chance we get. From the moment Summer entered the world, there were so many questions and struggles we would have to face and overcome. The lesson here is this: The things that challenge our faith make us stronger.

Summer puzzled the doctors. They were trying to find a syndrome to place her in, but never could. From jaundice, to infections, head too large—the list would go on. Every time we took her to the doctor, the conversation went something like this: "I would like for you to take her over to the hospital and let's run some more tests."

As time went on, it was trip after trip to doctors' offices. After so many hospital visits, as soon as we would drive into the parking lot, Summer would begin to cry. And there were notable accidents that occurred along the way. Once when we pastored our first church, she slipped and hit the back of her head on the bathroom ceramic-tile floor I had just mopped. The stabbing pain hurt so badly that when she screamed, she would stiffen her back and start turning blue from holding her breath.

No Diagnosis

The routine of hospital visits and tests became so exhausting. When the tests came back with negative results, they finally classed her as "failure to thrive"—which, when looking back at her life, makes no sense at all because she is a tough, determined little fighter! She has thrived and survived!

One Sunday, when Summer was eight months old, we didn't attend church because she was sick and running a fever. We ended up taking her to the emergency room after my husband preached. The doctors in Hinesville sent us directly to Memorial Hospital in Savannah, Georgia. While there, she was placed in the NICU because of her high fever and bulging fontanel (soft spot). The doctors mentioned it could possibly be *hydrocephalus* (fluid on the brain), so tests would be needed to determine exactly what was going on. They did a CT scan, a spinal tap, and other tests during the days that followed, but found nothing. Finally, they attributed her condition to be viral in nature.

I remember staying at the Ronald McDonald House while my husband stayed at home, pastoring our church, and taking care of Matthew. This house was such a blessing to have for a family to stay in such a nice place at no cost. I remember Jim and Kathy Milligan coming to see us; our state overseer, C. E. and Hazel Landreth, as well as other family and friends. Of course, members from our church supported us in so many ways.

Summer also had common surgeries and diagnoses. She had tubes placed in her ears from having so many nasty ear infections. The doctors believed this would help with her delay of speech as well as her balance. Then, a heart murmur was detected, which was determined to be *mitral valve prolapse*. This is when a valve doesn't close properly and requires echocardiograms (ultrasound) and electrocardiograms (ECG). Summer had to be given prophylactic antibiotics before surgery or a dental procedure to prevent possible infection. It sounds complicated, but not really—just another thing to add to the list.

As a result of all the tests coming back negative, she was finally classed as "developmentally delayed." Looking back, I see many things that could have indicated the AVM (arteriovenous malformation), but somehow nothing was ever mentioned—failure to thrive, a whooshing sound, mitral valve prolapse, or possible hydrocephalus. I am glad I didn't know. That would have been horrible to think every day, *Is this the day her brain will hemorrhage?* Yes, sometimes "ignorance is bliss."

More 'ER' Visits

At age three, Summer was referred to a pediatric neurologist in Savannah for her first of many MRIs. She was having trouble keeping food on her stomach. People around me might have thought my cologne didn't smell very good because I usually had puke on me. And it didn't matter where we were—church, Winterfest, camp meeting, General Assembly—it would happen. The vomiting was so aggressive that she would completely empty her stomach and then continue with dry heaves. These episodes always required medical attention. Our survival kit included Pedialyte for dehydration and plastic bags. If we had to fly, we would make sure to gather up our cute little airsickness bags and add to our collection.

People probably wondered why we didn't leave her at home with a caregiver, but by living away from our parents and family, it wasn't always possible. Since my parents were attending some of the same events, they wanted to see her. You know how those grandparents can be.

Once at Midwest Winterfest, we ended up at the hospital in Cincinnati, Ohio. Several times while attending the General Assembly, we would go out to eat with friends and end up at the emergency room. Our friends handled it well. They would go into a gift or souvenir store, buy her an outfit, call us a taxi, and off we would go. It usually took about six hours because the ER wouldn't let us leave until she stopped throwing up, was able to keep a Popsicle on her stomach, and could go to the bathroom.

Another Accident

While we were pastoring in Jesup, Georgia, Summer was throwing up and we ended up at the ER. While waiting for her to be treated, I walked the floors with her in my arms. Just as I walked past a huge wooden double door, someone came through so quickly that the door hit the side of her head very hard. She cried and they apologized . . . and we waited.

For a while, Summer continued to progress in every way and was doing really well. We were so thankful she didn't have to take medication. She made friends with everyone she met because of her sweet and loving disposition.

She enjoys riding her bike, which is actually an adult trike. While we were in South Carolina, she rode one until it literally fell apart. We have bought three new sets of tires and repaired chains, handlebars, and bent frames. Since we lived on the campground, she loved to ride and talk to our neighbors and anyone else she could stop. She got a lot of wonderful exercise and beautiful sunshine.

However, a few times she had severe accidents where she would have a seizure and it would cause her to wreck. We finally got her to wear a helmet. When we left the state, they gave her a brand-new fuchsia Miami Sun trike. She loves it, but she misses living on the campground and the association she had with all the people living close by. She learned their schedules, and when it was time for them to come home from school or work, she would be outside riding, hoping to get a chance to talk to them. Most of the time she would ask them to pray for her. No, I'm not talking about later during their nightly prayers, but right then and there in the extreme hot temperature, and they so graciously reciprocated. Since we no longer live on the campground, she doesn't enjoy riding as much. It's not nearly as much fun to ride now.

Unanswered Prayers

Has life changed for the Propes family? Indeed, it has. We are unable to do a lot of the things we used to do, and that is sad to me. Some days, Summer just doesn't feel well. She will even say, "I want Jesus to come get me now."

Even though some things are new, our faith in God remains the same because He never changes. There are so many unanswered questions I don't understand, but I have been raised to trust God. That's what I do.

Women my age are, for the most part, taking care of themselves; or, if they do find themselves in difficult places, all the responsibility may not rest solely on them. That's a good thing. Even though Summer is twenty-four years old, I still assist her every day with bath time, her food preparation, and any other needs she might have. It's like having a small child for a much longer period—combined with the drama and needs of a teenager. I realize there are reasons why we have our children when we are young! We need the energy for sure. Lattes and lavender-scented baths are simple things, yet sublime.

Through the years, I have been blessed to find good caregivers that allow me to do ministry with my husband or to just have special time together. I have said on several occasions that our date night included a funeral or a wedding. That's pitiful, I know, but things are better now, even though we are always conscious of our situation no matter how far we go.

I'm so grateful for every moment and each person who has entered our lives. God has always provided that special one. Sometimes I find myself trying to ensure the future and end up like the children of Israel, wanting more than one day's manna. But God provided enough manna for only one day. So, I surrender to Him and let faith carry me through those times of uncertainty. And enough "manna" (caregiver) is always there. He is so faithful and comes through for me—and He will for you, too!

Healthy Goals

One day I noticed I was losing more than normal amounts of hair. I started doing research and went to a couple of doctors, only to have them tell me, "Well, it could be stress."

"I don't feel stressed," I replied, "and besides, everyone has stress . . . it's called life."

What's stressful is losing your hair suddenly with no known reason or sickness.

After Summer was born, my thyroid gland became hyperactive. Of course, it took some time to figure out what was going on. All I know is that I could eat a lot of food and not gain weight. Now I have to admit I like that concept, but it was not healthy for my heart. My friend and I would make a short trip from Hinesville to Jesup to enjoy some pool time at her mother's house. On the way, we would stop at a convenience store and get a snack for now and one for later. Then a new Dairy Queen opened and we made a stop there, too.

Even though hyperthyroidism can cause hair loss, I didn't suspect this to be the reason because it wasn't a new diagnosis and my medication levels are checked every six months. So, what was the cause? Maybe it *was* stress.

We all know we can't control everything in our lives, but there are some things we can control. For me, it was to make sure I was taking care of myself as well as Summer. I needed to concentrate on things that would be beneficial to my body, mind, and spirit. I needed to be my best so I could give my best. Someone was depending on me.

After putting Summer in bed, it was easy and so enjoyable for me to grab a box of Cheez-Its and diet Dr. Pepper to relax while watching television. And if you know me well, you know I love sweets—especially donuts. But soon I realized I was only adding to my problems. I needed to eat well, get a good night's rest, and start exercising. I have always loved walking, and have done so even before Matthew was born; but when anyone gets overwhelmed with issues, the very thing that helps is the first thing to go. I needed to get back to the basics.

Summer also loves to eat and will eat anything—even sardines! It was easy for me to make healthy choices for her. I heard that food was like medicine, so we started eating properly and practicing portion control. Sometimes she will ask me, "Is that a lot?" I'm sure she's thinking, *It doesn't look like much to me.*

"Yes," I reply and, thankfully, she's satisfied with that. She was too little to carry extra weight. That alone could add more health issues to the insurmountable ones she was experiencing already. Over a two-year period, we lost about fifty pounds collectively. When I found ways to accomplish my three goals of eating healthier, getting more rest, and exercising, I did better—and so did my hair.

MAJOR CHALLENGES

Ten Things Only Women Understand

Social media provides so many great quotes and funny stories that friends send to each other. Certain things, I'm convinced, can only be understood by the female gender. Men in general cannot comprehend the concept of eating half a salad for lunch and drinking a diet drink so you can order cheesecake for dessert.

Recently, I received the following list of things in an email (source unknown) that only women can understand and appreciate:

10. Cats' facial expressions

9. The need for the same style of shoes in different colors

8. Why bean sprouts aren't just weeds

7. Fat clothes

6. Taking a car trip without trying to beat your best time

5. The difference between beige, off-white, and eggshell

4. Cutting your bangs to make them grow

3. Eyelash curlers

2. The inaccuracy of every bathroom scale ever made

[And the number one thing only women understand:]
1. Other women

Many Visitors

Looking back, I remember how quiet the hospital was on that Memorial Day weekend when Summer had her stroke. We were placed on the fourth floor, which was for outpatient surgery, and there was no one else there. So we set up "house" on this beautiful floor. I would straighten magazines, throw people's trash away, make sure the chairs were aligned properly, and answer all the phones that rang. It was wonderful to have such a nice place for all our loved ones to visit. And being like my mother, I made sure everyone had what they needed—trying to entertain and be a good hostess. The Pink Ladies said they were going to miss me when I was gone.

Soon, trying to stay busy and entertaining the visitors became exhausting. There was a continuous stream of people coming and going. It wasn't their fault; it was mine. This was a place I had never been before. I've never been in the hospital myself other than to have my babies. These precious people just wanted us to know they cared, and, if I had it to do over, I wouldn't change a thing. Some wanted to talk, some would sit quietly, and others would cry. We did it all with them. Their presence meant so much.

We didn't have access to social media like we do today. I should be grateful because I'm not sure I could have kept up. I don't even remember having a cell phone. I always got Matthew's hand-me-downs, and I think he still had his first phone at that time. I do remember three phones (maybe they were pay phones) that sat side by side in the waiting area. Sometimes they would all ring at the same time and our friends would take turns helping me answer them.

A Pretty Smile

When Summer was about four years old, she had hospital dentistry due to severe decay of several primary teeth. Being a registered dental hygienist, I was well aware of the problems with baby-bottle tooth decay, so Summer was off the bottle early and she never took it to bed. However, because of being underweight, she would get up at night and I would feed her vanilla pudding. What was I thinking? That was so much worse than a bottle of milk.

Sometimes, educated people make poor decisions, and this was certainly one of those times. So, at Tallahassee Memorial Hospital in Florida, she had eight crowns put on her baby teeth. This procedure was important for several reasons: Those teeth needed to remain in place to hold a space for her permanent teeth and make sure she didn't have pain and infection. The crowns also assured that she would be able to chew properly. She did really well except for being sick from the anesthesia, and today she has pretty and healthy teeth. She loves going to the dentist and having them cleaned. So do I!

Stages of Growth

God has taught me many lessons in the past eleven years since Summer had the stroke. One very important lesson I've learned is that all our difficulties have a purpose . . . and they are not in vain. We may go through times when our faith is tested, but that's when we must plant the seed of God's Word in our hearts. In nature, just as a seed has to remain in the ground to germinate, so the Word of God has to abide in us.

Mark 4:26-29 describes the process:

Jesus also said, "The Kingdom of God is like a farmer who scatters seed on the ground. Night and day, while he's asleep or awake, the seed sprouts and grows, but he does not understand how it happens. The earth produces the crops on its own. First a leaf blade pushes through, then the heads of wheat are formed, and finally the grain ripens. And as soon as the grain is ready, the farmer comes and harvests it with a sickle, for the harvest time has come" (NLT).

Planting a seed is not enough to assure a harvest. The seed must be protected and taken care of until harvest time. If the seed is dug up or not watered, it will not produce. As much as we would like to, we cannot bypass the growth cycle and get the harvest right now. From seed time to harvest we go through stages of planting, weeding, and cultivating. The full harvest comes, and then there is emptiness again. We can't live in the sunshine all the time. If our lives were perfect here, we wouldn't want to go to heaven.

SHE'S A CUTIE . . .   SHE'S ALSO A MESS!

A SOMBER MOMENT

OUR FAMILY 1998

GROWING UP

FOUR MONTHS AFTER
THE HEMORRHAGE

RIDING HER MIAMI SUN TRIKE

CHAPTER FOUR

*Weeping may endure for a night, but joy
cometh in the morning.*

—Psalm 30:5 KJV

MY DESERT EXPERIENCE

THE UPS AND DOWNS OF SUMMER'S DIFFERENT MEDICATIONS (and the inevitable side effects of each), the unexpected turns of her unstable moods, and the unpredictable trauma of generalized seizures may resemble a "roller coaster" ride in the park. But that is where the similarity ends. This was certainly no joy ride—quite the opposite. I cannot imagine what her tiny body has endured for years, but the joy and strength she exudes is unbelievable.

Nehemiah 8:10 reminds me: "Do not grieve, for the joy of the Lord is your strength." But I felt like my life had stalled in "neutral," and I was stuck on a hot and arid desert with no oasis in sight. I share Summer's journey and my own "desert" experience because it helps to hear of others' tough times and know there *are* victories along the way.

One devotion I read explained the dilemma this way: "As we contend with our own desert experiences, it helps to have something concrete in someone else's desert to hang onto. To know that while our experiences are unique to us, the realm of the desert is something that we all experience, one way or another."

Recently I read that one-third of earth's land surface is comprised of deserts. When we think of the desert, the first thing that comes to mind is the sand, the heat, or the scaly lizard called the Gila monster. The old television cartoons also come to mind where Speedy Gonzales leads his unsuspecting predators into a cactus. Ouch! That's how my desert experience has been—prickly and unpredictably painful.

Desert Flowers

To my surprise, there are magnificent desert wildflowers that grow in abundance in Arizona and Southern California. It is estimated that around eight hundred to two thousand species of cacti also grow in the desert. The *barrel cactus*—man-sized or bigger—is a cylinder-type plant that has numerous parallel ridges on the side and is topped with sharp three- to four-inch spines. Surprisingly, the barrel cactus is also a flowering plant with beautiful rings of yellow-green or red blossoms at the top.

Like many plants of the world, this cactus has numerous uses, including food. Native Americans in the southwest part of America stewed the barrel cactus to make a cabbage-like food. They got water to drink from the pulp and they made fish hooks from the pointed spines. The pulp can also be made into cactus candy. Yum!

Rich Blessings

Can you see the picture? As I've grown spiritually through this loathsome desert of caring for Summer and her needs, God's Word has matured me with "blossoms" of rich blessings. Among the many people who came to pray for Summer, I remember a beautiful African-American lady evangelist praying for her while she was still in ICU. She "spoke" to the right side, which was paralyzed since surgery, with authority based on God's Word, and Summer began to move her right side before our eyes. As prayer continued, the miracle continued.

Almost eleven years have passed since we entered that dark desert filled with surgeries, seizures, and multiple medications—and the journey is ongoing. Through it all, I am reminded so often of God's faithfulness and His sovereignty. We know our desert did not catch God by surprise. Summer is alive; she knows who we are, and she is able to communicate with us. Is she completely healed? Not yet . . . but she continues to grow stronger each day, and we hold to the promise in Romans 8:35-39:

> Who shall separate us from the love of Christ? Shall trouble or hardship or persecution or famine or nakedness or danger or sword? . . . No, in all these things we are more than conquerors through him who loved us. For I am convinced that neither death nor life, neither angels nor demons, neither the present nor the future, nor any powers, neither height nor depth, nor anything else in all creation, will be able to separate us from the love of God that is in Christ Jesus our Lord.

While we were traveling across the country evangelizing, we made a record album. The year was 1981, eight years prior to Summer's birth, and it was titled *More Than Conquerors*.

The following message is written on the back cover:

The apostle Paul declared centuries ago, "In all these things we are more than conquerors through him that loved us." If any disciple of Christ ever really "knew Him in the fellowship of His sufferings," Paul did. Yet, in the midst of trouble, persecution, turmoil, and pain, Paul cries out, "We've been made more than conquerors through Christ Jesus our Lord!" And my dear friends, as you listen to LaQuita sing the title song, I want you to realize that you can make it. When you feel lonely and depressed, let the song "I Can Call on Jesus Anytime" lift you up and set you free!

Here are three things I want you to remember: God is your source, God is bigger than any problem, and God is ready, willing, and abundantly able to supply your every need!

It is my prayer that this, our very first album, will bless, inspire, and encourage you to reach for deeper depths and higher heights in Jesus Christ our Lord.

With Love, Tommy

These were words we had been taught all our lives. Church is all we knew. And, yes, we believed them. Now as we live them, we still believe.

Making a Difference

When we click on the nightly news, we see children who are hurting, and we realize they are crying out for help. Whether it is a visible, physical illness or one that's not so visible, we must be attentive to their cry. We can make a difference.

Educators—whether in school or church—give so much, and I am so grateful for their dedication. And while caring for a special-needs child is challenging on many levels, I'm sure it is rewarding. I have noticed how some have dealt with Summer, and what a blessing it was for the parents as well as the child. And best of all, the children feel the tender, loving care they give.

A Detour

God continued to change the journey with unexpected detours. In 2005, at T.C. Thompson Children's in Chattanooga, Tennessee, Summer had to have a *vagus nerve stimulator* (VNS) implanted, which is similar to a pacemaker. A small device was implanted under the skin near the collarbone with a wire that connects the device to the vagus nerve in her neck. After the implant is in place, the doctor programs it to produce weak electrical signals that travel along the vagus nerve to the brain at regular intervals. These signals help prevent the electrical bursts in the brain that cause seizures.

It was outpatient surgery, so we weren't expected to be there too long. Dr. Bill George came to visit. Through the years, he has proven to be a friend to our family, and we were delighted to see him. However, Summer had a reaction to the anesthesia and her body was flailing around; she was screaming, and there was nothing we could do about it. I hated for his visit to be disrupted, but Dr. George didn't seem to notice.

Later that year, the neurologist wanted to do a video monitoring that would require a week's stay at Emory Hospital in Atlanta, Georgia. During this procedure, the EEG is recorded for a prolonged period, accompanied by continuous closed-circuit video observation. The digitized EEG and recorded behavior are displayed simultaneously, allowing point-to-point correlations of recorded events and any accompanying electrographic changes.

During the week, the neurologist gradually reduced her seizure meds to induce seizures and record them. Summer could only move about six feet from her bed for the entire week. At one point, they needed to go deeper into the brain, so they inserted a steel wire in the side of her face with no anesthesia. That was heart-wrenching. They recorded many seizures and even a generalized one. We were so ready to go home. What a week!

In 2006, we would face a second brain surgery, and we would go through some of the same things again. Was it easier the second time around? Not at all. No parent is ever prepared to cuddle a hurting child.

Encouragers

While we were living in Cleveland, Tennessee, and my husband was the general director of publications for the Church of God, we received so many well-wishes from the employees, including Dr. Bill George, editor in chief; Pauline Justice, my husband's assistant; as well as the Executive Committee and the Women's Ministries Department.

Prior to leaving for surgery, we visited International Offices, and Summer had her photo taken in the general overseer's chair. Dr. Dennis McGuire was always a fan. Then we stopped by and saw Dr. Mary Ruth Stone and all the precious ladies in the Women's Ministries Department. They gave her a duffle bag that she used on our trip to Atlanta, for surgery and every trip since!

The doctors thought that if they went back into the brain and did some cleanup surgery, it would help abort seizures. Summer was admitted to Egleston Children's Hospital again, where they opened the same area to remove scar tissue and hopefully eliminate seizures. This time, they removed the entire hippocampus in the left temporal lobe. The surgeon said that if he had gone any further, she would have been blind in her left eye. Her peripheral vision is severely compromised.

So, here we went through some of the same painful experiences all over again. The surgery was unsuccessful.

Summer had a seizure that night in ICU, and we were devastated.

Our church family stuck with us. Again, God's Word was our rock and shield, guiding us through the desert with encouragement from 1 Corinthians 12:22-25:

> Those parts of the body that seem to be weaker are indispensable, and the parts that we think are less honorable we treat with special honor. And the parts that are unpresentable are treated with special modesty, while our presentable parts need no special treatment. But God has put the body together, giving greater honor to the parts that lacked it, so that there should be no division in the body, but that its parts should have equal concern for each other.

Those who have been with us through stages of this journey are loved and appreciated more than you know. The attention and care you gave us are life-saving, not only for Summer but also for other family members.

An Angel Unaware

I don't know about you, but I think in a straight line. Since childhood, structure and routine are my friends. I appreciate clearly defined outlines, itineraries, maps, and step-by-step instructions for assembling items that come in pieces. When I find myself examining the pieces of my life,

A SUMMER STORY
OF GOD'S ENDURING GRACE

I wonder, *How in the world does all of this fit together?* In his best-selling book *The Journey of Desire*, John Eldredge says, "The more comfortable you are with the mystery in the journey, the more rest you will know along the way."

When I was eleven years old, my mother had a child late in life and, because her health was in danger, the doctors took the baby at six months. LaJuana, my baby sister, was born October 5, 1967, weighing three pounds, two ounces. A lot has changed since the '60s, but then the doctors didn't give her much chance of survival. She had many birth complications that made her future look dim.

I remember it all quite well. My mother was in the hospital three weeks, but my dad took very good care of my brother and me. I remember going to school only a few times with tangles in my long blonde hair.

It was touch-and-go for a while; one day LaJuana would be up half an ounce, and the next day she would lose a pound. She remained in the hospital 110 days. My parents went to the hospital every day to learn how to feed her and take care of her until the day they finally got to bring her home. The doctors reminded them that even though she had lived longer than expected, she would never survive the exposure to the outside germs and sickness. We were so excited and we wanted all our friends to see her. My mom told us we were blessed to have LaJuana as part of our family. She taught us many things in life that could never be learned from a book—and I agree.

Her physical body and mental condition were severely impaired; she had dim vision, curvature of the spine, and never walked or talked, but she spoke volumes to us. Over her little lifespan, she had eight sets of casts on her legs and three sets of braces, so carrying her was difficult. Even though LaJuana never spoke, she had a way of getting our attention. She would knock on the wall with her cast. If that didn't work, she would bang a little louder. Then when you got to the door, she would just smile the biggest grin ever.

Some children with issues of this magnitude would be homebound, but LaJuana traveled all over the country in an RV with my parents as they evangelized. No matter how long they had been away from home, as soon as they would make the turn to their house and go over the railroad track, she would giggle and get so excited! She knew she was home.

My mother kept many notes about LaJuana, and in between those writings she recorded, "Since my last entry, my little girl went to be with the Lord December 7, 1979."

One of my mom's favorite books was *Angel Unaware*, by Dale Evans. Entertainers Roy and Dale Evans Rogers were thrilled when their little daughter Robin was born. But their excitement turned to concern when they were informed that Robin was born with Down syndrome and they were advised to "put her away." The Rogers ignored such talk and, instead, kept Robin. She graced their home for two and a half years. Though Robin's time on earth was short, she changed her parents' lives and even made life better for other children born with special needs in the years to come.

Angel Unaware is Robin's account of her life as she looks down from heaven. As she speaks to God about the mission of love she just completed on earth, the reader sees how she brought her parents closer to God and encouraged them to help other children in need. This book changed the way America treated children with special needs, and is still available to a new generation. It is the perfect gift for parents of special-needs children, parents grieving the death of a child, or anyone whose life has been touched by a special child.

LaJuana's gravestone is inscribed with, "An Angel With a Mission Completed." I think Dale Evans would love that.

In the early '80s, I wrote an article that was printed in the *Church of God Evangel*. It included a poem written by my best friend's mother, and I believe it truly captures LaJuana's twelve years on earth.

Fair hair blooming, she races through the grass,

Jumping rope, playing ball, singing "Home at Last"

Gathering flowers on a hillside that has no end

Laughing, skipping, whispering to a newfound friend.

MY DESERT EXPERIENCE

Hands outstretched, she climbs the golden stair,

Eyes flashing in anticipation, for Jesus awaits her there.

She bows in worship as He takes her by the hand.

She praises Him for lending her to earthy woman and man.

Then kneeling humbly at His feet, a question she does ask,

Did I please You, Lord? Did I complete my task?

I wanted to come home, but I loved my family so.

Tell me, Lord, were they really strong enough for me to go?

In loving-kindness the One who knoweth all then speaks,

And gives her the answers that with all her heart she seeks.

My child, you did your job so well, your work on earth is done,

Your loved ones are now strong enough, My work to carry on.

So rest now, darling daughter, and know without a doubt

If ever they have a problem, their Lord will bring them out.

For now they have more reason, the gospel words to say,

There's more to come to heaven for than they had yesterday!

—Cherrie Ard

What a glorious reunion that's going to be!

Many Twists and Turns

God chooses to take us down paths we do not understand and by ways we do not know, because He is building our character and making us more like Him. Our part is to trust Him when the way is unclear, the reasons are unexplained, and we absolutely cannot trace His hand no matter how hard we try. I've learned that, in those moments when we have the least control, God has the most control. He is at work in our lives in ways we could never imagine or dream. The situations in our lives all build on each other. Life is not a series of many continuous journeys—it is one long journey with many twists, turns, and desert experiences.

Perhaps your period of waiting is God's way of showing you He doesn't want you to seek answers—He wants you to seek Him. In God's time, your unanswered questions will be answered. In the meantime, He wants you to have a faith that gives Him everything, even when the way is not clear and the outcome is unknown.

Many times, His answers lie hidden in the midst of the very circumstance that is bringing us grief or stress. Those answers can be uncovered only by those who choose to look for the hand of God in everything and say, "Lord, I don't understand this turn in the road, but I'll go where You lead me. I know Your plan is perfect and You are far more qualified than I am to orchestrate the events of my life."

MY DESERT EXPERIENCE

When treading through life's desert, it helps me to remember God's help in my past experiences. Though I may not know you by name, I'm certain that if you're not in a desert experience at this very moment, the time is sure to come. When that day arrives, you will not face it unarmed. The Bible, sharper than any two-edged sword, contains desert psalms that can become your battle cry.

Read the words, or sing the inspiring chorus (if you know the tune) to Fanny Crosby's hymn, "He Hideth My Soul":

> He hideth my soul in the cleft of the rock
>
> That shadows a dry, thirsty land,
>
> He hideth my life in the depths of His love,
>
> And covers me there with His hand.

Be reminded that close by your side will be a faithful, powerful God who has only good plans for you—plans that lead to spiritual victory and "joy in the morning."

ALBUM COVER (1981)

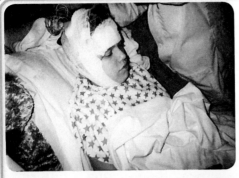

VIDEO
MONITORING,
2005

SITTING IN THE GENERAL OVERSEER'S CHAIR

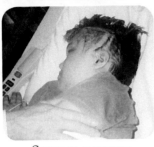

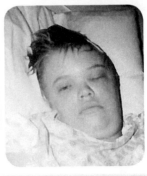

SECOND SURGERY
2006

CHAPTER FIVE

*He that dwelleth in the secret place of
the most High shall abide under the
shadow of the Almighty.
I will say of the Lord, He is my refuge
and my fortress: my God;
in him will I trust.*

—Psalm 91:1-2 KJV

A FATHER'S PERSPECTIVE

A TRAUMATIC ILLNESS LIKE THE ONE SUMMER EXPERIENCED on Memorial Day weekend in 2002, and the likelihood that she might not survive, affects every member of the family—especially the parents. This chapter is devoted to providing a background narrative of a father who walked "through the valley of the shadow" filled with fear, doubt, and despair to eventually find healing in the secret dwelling place of the Almighty.

From My Heart

Those were dark days. I remember telling several people: "I would never wish this on the meanest man in the world." In life, we expect the death of our grandparents. Then, at different times, it's normal to assume that we will bury our parents. In most cases, one spouse will die before the other. But we are not genetically programmed to be able to rationally deal with the death of our children. It's the most heart-breaking thing a parent can imagine. During those first twenty-four to forty-eight hours when it appeared that Summer would not survive, it was like I went into a suspended animation and found myself stuck in an emotional "overdrive" of despair. This was my baby girl, and I was not prepared to face her possible death.

My Background

I am a blessed man! This is not a trite statement. I have often said: "God has been better to me than I would have been to myself."

"How is that?" you might ask.

Let me explain. Born in a small mill town in southeast Georgia, I am a fourth-generation Church of God member. As an only child, I was raised in and around church. I was told that I cut my teeth on the old "Red-back" *Church Hymnal.* We were Pentecostal to the core—you know, before it was "cool" to be Pentecostal. My mother was of the "old time" holiness brand. The only thing she ever put on her face was water and Ivory soap, followed up by Noxzema skin cream. I remember when she stopped pulling her hair back in a small bun and progressed to the updo beehive hair-do. She struggled with that transition for a while. I heard her tell someone that she didn't want to "grieve the Holy Ghost" by changing her hairstyle too much. I know that sounds simple and antiquated; but, you see, she meant that—she lived it every day regardless. That was who she was. The beauty of her testimony was this: she didn't legislate her convictions on anyone else. With an open and loving heart, she would quickly say, "Honey, these are my convictions. This is what the Lord convicted me of." She was a fortress of righteousness and faith.

My dad was a truck driver. His limited church background was southern Methodist, but he never really made a profession of faith until 1965. We were attending a service during an Oral Roberts Crusade in Charleston, South Carolina, and that night my father was, as the old-timers used to say, "gloriously saved." I was eight years old. The reason I know he really got saved was because he started paying tithes. That's the way I was raised—in a loving, Christian home.

You see, I don't have a dramatic testimony of God rescuing me from a rebellious lifestyle of drugs, alcohol, or other things teenagers can get involved with. Thankfully, my parents never had to bail me out of jail or enroll me in any type of rehab program. Church was my life.

So, when I say I was raised "close," I mean just that— I was raised close to God, His people, and His Church. That's my roots.

During my teen years, a big event for me was to be able to attend a district youth rally. I attended one in Macon, Georgia, in the mid-70s and experienced a life-changing event: I met LaQuita. I was stricken by her beauty—inside and out. At the time, I was working at a music store in Warner Robins, Georgia, selling instruments and being trained to teach music. Although I have never considered myself a gifted musician, music has been a big influence in my life and would later become an avenue of healing to my troubled heart and soul.

After LaQuita and I married in 1976, we moved to Valdosta, Georgia, where we worked at the Forrest Street Church of God with Pastor J. R. Chambers. At first, I didn't feel the call to preach, so I was credentialed as a licensed minister of music. When I told Pastor Chambers that I felt a call to pulpit ministry, he encouraged me to attend Lee College (now Lee University). "You have a God-given talent," he said, "and you've done well, but you need more formal training. Go to Lee for at least a year and get Lee's name behind your ministry."

Lee Days

In fall of 1977, we moved to Cleveland, Tennessee. That's where I fell in love again—this time with Christian education. My major professor, Martin Baldree, became my academic hero. He taught me so much about the discipline of Christian education that I thought, *This is where I'll spend my ministry. I can do this!*

LaQuita worked at Lee in the Title III Program. I worked with T. A. Perkins at the Daisy (Tennessee) Church of God as an associate, leading music and doing anything else the pastor needed me to do. I worked hard, took maximum academic loads, and finished a four-year degree in two years and nine months. I wanted to be the best Christian education director in the Church of God. That was my goal, but God had other plans.

Ministry Days

Rather than experiencing a dramatic "Damascus road" experience like the apostle Paul, my call to pulpit ministry evolved. After graduating from Lee, LaQuita and I evangelized. After preaching my very first sermon, I was bitten with the "preaching bug." With this "bite," we moved back to South Georgia and evangelized for almost five years. Then I was appointed to the Live Oak Church of God in Hinesville, Georgia, and stayed there nearly nine years.

This was an exciting time of ministry. God favored us and we saw phenomenal growth in the Army-based military town. God blessed our time there. During our last year, according to the records, we averaged more than six hundred in Sunday morning worship attendance. When I felt like my time was finished there, I went back into evangelistic work. After sixteen months of evangelizing, State Overseer Junus Fulbright appointed us to the Jesup, Georgia, Church of God. We stayed there one year and then we were appointed as state overseer to the Great Lakes Region. I was thirty-six years old.

We had four tremendous years in the Great Lakes Region and then we were appointed to serve as state overseer of Northern Ohio for six years. Although the ministry there was absolutely wonderful, that's where my world collapsed. It was, as they say, "the best of times and the worst of times!" I was not prepared to face the darkness that I, as a father, was about to enter.

A FATHER'S PERSPECTIVE

Summer Joy

Let me describe the beautiful child, born March 2, 1989, we appropriately named *Summer Joy*. Her sparkling personality was evident from a young age. She could light up any room; she loved everyone, and everyone loved her! At that time she had no serious health issues, only a slight developmental delay. She was doing well.

Suddenly, on May 25, 2002, without warning, Summer suffered a near-fatal cerebral hemorrhage. Her left temporal lobe burst due to an arteriovenous malformation. Initially, the doctors were not optimistic that she would recover. When I asked her neurosurgeon what was the worst case he had seen, he pointed over his shoulder and said concerning Summer, "She is the worst I've ever seen!" My world was collapsing, and I felt helpless to save our little girl.

The entire family became absorbed in adapting to Summer's traumatic situation. Friends and church associates were there for us. Any time a member of the family suffers a sudden and chronic illness, the task of 24/7 care is overwhelming. First, you deal with the shock and then discover you have to adapt to all the different medicines, doctors' appointments, and special diets. It changes the way you live. If you're not careful, your life is consumed with the care and well-being of your child, and the entire family can be negatively affected.

A Dark Place

During this time, my ministry never suffered or slowed. I continued to work every day, supervised the construction of a new office complex and ministry center in Akron (Ohio), traveled, and preached every weekend. Everything looked normal, but it wasn't.

After a year and a half following Summer's stroke, I went into a deep, dark place emotionally. In my ministry, I prayed for people who were miraculously healed, but in my "private place," I was sick and sinking into a dark emotional abyss. For the first time in my life, I questioned God! I simply could not understand how all of this had come to our home, to our family. I was in trouble and didn't know what to do about it. Everything I had believed and preached my entire ministry was upside down.

This was new territory for me. Unable to sleep or eat, I lost thirty pounds in two months. Looking back, I was probably standing at the precipice of depression, but at the time, I couldn't put a label on it. I remember once asking my assistant, Barbara Henderson, "How can a Holy Ghost-filled person be depressed?" Obviously, I hadn't lived long enough or been through enough at that point to understand, but oh, how quickly that all changed.

God's Word

The Twenty-third Psalm, a passage of Scripture I knew from childhood, became so real to me. I learned what it meant to "walk through the valley of the shadow of death," but I also learned that it was much easier to doubt than to practice the faith I was preaching.

My valley of the shadow lasted six and a half months. I would get up very early in the morning, read Psalm 91 aloud while walking back and forth in my basement, pleading with God to help me . . . help Summer . . . help us! As I would read the chapter, I'd say, "God, if You're listening, this is YOUR Word . . . these are YOUR promises; now what are YOU going to do about it?"

You see, in my younger days, I was one of those high-powered evangelists always preaching on faith, miracles, and divine healing. Now it seemed that God was requiring me to "walk out" and actually "live by" what I had always preached to others. That was hard to do. I could not comprehend the condition I was in. I remember making the statement one time, "God has preserved me," because I never had any major problems; I had lived a blessed life! But here I was. Life had hit me and my family so very hard, and heaven was silent.

My Healing

Although music was in my background, I had never listened much to worship music outside of the church setting. My sweet wife, LaQuita, encouraged me to listen to a tape of the West Angeles Church of God in Christ Mass Choir singing praise music. So, loving their music, I did. One song here, two songs there, and then the whole tape, over and over again. This started the breakthrough I was seeking. Theologically, I don't know how to explain fully what I was going through. Even though I was doing effective ministry, I so needed healing myself. This praise music, plus reading aloud the Word of God, started bringing me out of this dark valley. In a few months, I was whole again, stable, and had a made-up mind that, like my mother used to say, "I will trust Him no matter what!"

Let me be bold here for a minute: If my mother is not in heaven, heaven is a myth. She walked and talked with God. Even when she was wasting away in a care facility dying from the dreaded disease of Alzheimer's, one of the last things she ever said to me was a reply to an eternal question I asked her, "Mama, can I trust Him?"

"Honey, you can trust Him to the bitter end." That was remarkable! I never really had her back again. I believe her response was a message God sent me.

This journey has been long and hard. However, each day we live we are trusting God for a full recovery and complete healing for Summer. We are grateful for the medical team and faithful caregivers who assist us in providing the ongoing care that Summer needs. But at the end of each day, she, like the rest of us, is held in the grip of God's mighty hand. He will determine her future, and I am convinced it will be good. How do I know that? Jeremiah 29:11 declares, "For I know the thoughts that I think toward you, says the Lord, thoughts of peace and not of evil, to give you a future and a hope" (NKJV)!

The fact is, Summer belongs to God. He allows us to love her and look after her, but she belongs to Him. He will see to her; with that, I choose to put my trust in Him.

CHAPTER SIX

In family life, love is the oil that eases friction, the cement that binds closer together, and the music that brings harmony.

—Eva Burrows

REFLECTIONS

Summer has been blessed to have a wonderful brother, Matthew, who is her supporter and ally. She loves him and his wife, Jennifer, knowing they are always there for her. Matthew has been a great son and brother to Summer, and we are so proud of him and his accomplishments.

We have discovered that a serious illness of any type affects every family member and becomes their central focus. This means the people who are not sick suffer, too. But Matthew never complained or acted as if he was neglected. Our schedule had to remain flexible, and Matthew always seemed to understand there were times when only some of us could attend one of his ballgames. God knew we would need him to be understanding, and he brings so much happiness into our lives. His name actually means "Gift of God," and he truly has been.

As you read Matthew's and Jennifer's reflections, you will understand more fully the journey our family has traversed.

Matthew—Summer's Brother

By my estimation, the beginning of my sibling relationship with Summer was relatively normal. The disparity between our ages and levels of development and maturity did not manifest until later in our lives. Consequently, we engaged and interacted as most siblings do—with all the requisite laughing, arguing, tattling, and sibling harassment that comes with the territory. Thankfully, our parents were never too far away and we were able to stay out of *excessive* mischief.

A sibling has a perspective slightly less central than a parent's, yet uniquely positioned for maximum insight into the life of an individual. Like so many other siblings, I was there for the formative moments in Summer's life. I was there, with sibling disdain, as her capability to grasp concepts and circumstances was sometimes underestimated by others, and I was there as her wit and natural sense of humor brightened our days. I was there, like a talent scout, to discover her ability to throw a ball with unanticipated strength and accuracy, as well as her ability to hit an underhand pitch without using a tee. I was there to see her display those talents in her Challenger League Baseball games. She was able to participate in the groundbreaking of the league's new state-of-the-art field, which was designed for special-needs children. The event was covered by local news stations, and cameras caught a glimpse of Summer during the ceremony. I was only asked to be her "Buddy" one time (the players had a Buddy who accompanied them in the field). Apparently, I was a better talent scout than a Buddy. Nonetheless, I was quite proud of her baseball aptitude and supported her endeavor from a distance.

Also, I was there on May 25, 2002, when our family was changed forever. I was in the basement on the Gibson website window-shopping for instruments. As the sounds of distress emanated from the upper floors, it was apparent that this was not a normal bout of illness with Summer. I could hear the urgency in my mother's voice, and the decision was quickly made to call 911. I went outside to direct the ambulance to our driveway, and the paramedics rushed upstairs. As they rolled Summer down the stairs and toward the door, the paramedic at the head of the gurney told her to tell her brother good-bye. We would later learn that the chief paramedic had no expectation for Summer to make it through the night.

Not quite two weeks later, I was there to visit Summer in the Intensive Care Unit. Uncertainty was the order of the day. There were no guarantees that she would recognize me or be able to communicate adequately. As I leaned over the rail, she opened her eyes from sleeping, and immediately started sobbing. She cried out in broken speech, "Matthew, I love you!" It was a little misty in the ICU that day.

Lastly, I was there when Summer came home. It was wonderful to see the work of God who miraculously brought her from the brink of death and back home at a pace that marveled even the doctors. She is a walking testimony of the fact that, even though life is not always ideal, we still serve a God who heals and holds our lives in the palm of His hand.

Many times I have said that Summer is the toughest member of our family. Seizures, invasive treatments, medication, a brain hemorrhage, and even the occasional minor bicycle crash, have all been unable to keep her down. Through all she has endured, she still epitomizes the *joy* of the Lord evoked by her middle name.

REFLECTIONS

Jennifer—Summer's "Best Sister"

When I began dating Matthew in 2006, Summer instantly became the little sister I never had. From our first meeting, she showed me what a true and beautiful little heart she had. Her welcomes were full of hugs and excited chatter, no matter if I had just seen her the day before or if it had been a small stretch of time.

When Matthew and I married in 2007, it was so heartwarming to me that she was thrilled to be gaining me as a "sister" into the Propes family. I was equally excited because I had learned what a gift she was to her (and now my) family. Not only did she provide a hug or smile when we came to see them, but she showed me what it was to see someone who accepted everything at face value. Summer takes people at their word!

Summer and I have a special relationship. When I call her on the phone, I know the point in the conversation when she'd like for me to pray for her. I'm glad to do so, because I know she believes the Lord can heal and help her. She's serious about her prayers and doesn't forget each night before she goes to bed. I also know that at some point in the conversation, either she or I will comment, "You are my best sister." When Matthew and I send her mail, it is one of the highlights of her day. She definitely knows when a piece of mail has her name on it!

If we could realize the things we can learn from the blessings God places in our lives, I believe we could stop taking certain things for granted. I love Summer Joy and am so thankful for the sweet words of affirmation she has spoken to me, the hugs she's blessed me with, and the heart of love she's opened up to me. I know she will always be my "best sister."

A Special Friend

One of my friends from Georgia, Kim Flournoy, dropped everything in her life and flew to Ohio to be with us, with no known date to fly back. She was such a blessing, and she kept everything lively. However, she is not a likely one to be talking with the Executive Committee members. She would tell me who called, and I would say with trepidation, "Kim, he is the general overseer!" Dr. Lamar Vest was the seated general. He's such a gracious man.

"Yes, I know," she would say, "and we are on first-name basis." I would have to smile, because to know her is to love her. I'm sure the entire committee and others enjoyed talking with her.

Kim became an important part of our family years before when she visited our church. Later, we had the distinct privilege of sharing with her the most precious gift of all—a baby. She and her husband, Jimmy, had been married ten years and didn't have any children, so they helped us with ours. When a call came asking if we wanted a baby girl, the answer was "Yes!" I called Kim, and our direction was clear. My husband and I, along with Kim, went to pick the baby up when she was less than twenty-four hours old. Today she is twenty-two, a graduate of the University of Georgia, and studying to be a pharmacist (God knew we would need one of those). While at UGA, she was captain of the majorettes, and during football season it was a Saturday tradition to watch Georgia play on College GameDay! Summer would put on her Bulldogs T-shirt and we would watch for the majorettes to come on the big screen. Many times we would text during the game. It was so much fun. Summer doesn't understand why football season isn't year round. We have been blessed to be the godparents of this sweet angel. Did I mention her name? It's Angel.

The Alphabet Prayer

Although life is a struggle
Because of pain and unexplained circumstances,

A SUMMER STORY
OF GOD'S ENDURING GRACE

Continue to be thankful.

Do not blame your problems on God

Even when you feel like giving up.

Fierce weather will gust at times, but

God is always faithful, so

Hold fast to His promises,

Inviting His love and

Joy to cover your life.

Keep praising Him for all His blessing and the

Love you have received in the past.

Magnify His name, knowing

No weapon formed against you

On earth will succeed.

Pause for a moment and

Quit doubting God's Word.

Reflect on the good times and

Share them with those you love.

Thank God for future blessings

Ushering in His presence with

Victory and celebration.

Welcome the opportunity to run the race with gratitude,

Xalting the great "I Am."

Yes, there will be a rainbow

Zooming with brilliance in that land of perfect rest!

SUMMER AND MATTHEW

MATTHEW AND JENNIFER

ANGEL ON
THE BIG SCREEN

UGA GAME

CHAPTER SEVEN

*To all who mourn in Israel, he will give
a crown of beauty for ashes, a joyous
blessing instead of mourning, festive
praise instead of despair.
In their righteousness, they will be like
great oaks that the Lord has planted
for his own glory.*

—Isaiah 61:3 NLT

CELEBRATIONS!

MEMORIAL DAY WILL ALWAYS HAVE MORE MEANING TO ME than a day of remembering the men and women who died while serving in the armed services. The year after Summer's stroke, we celebrated Matthew's high school graduation on Memorial Day weekend. It was a joyous occasion with an open-house party. Ohioans know how to do it right, and I love the idea because you get to see all your family and friends at one large gathering. Because it rained that weekend (does it always rain on Memorial Day?), we rented a big white tent for the back yard and had a Southern-style barbecue. The ground was a little soggy, but the tent held. With my son being such a patriot, we used red, white, and blue décor and it went nicely with the holiday. Incidentally, these are also the school colors for the Revere High Minutemen. Perfect! Happy memories!

Daystar Interview

Ten years after Summer's brush with death, we traveled on Memorial Day to Dallas, Texas, to appear on Daystar's *Celebration* program with Marcus and Joni Lamb. What a privilege and a blessing to be able to share our story on the second-largest and fastest-growing Christian Television Network in the world. Daystar has over 100 TV stations, with satellite and cable coverage that reaches more than 100 million U.S. households and more than 200 countries and 680 million households globally—with a potential coverage of two billion people. That's a lot of people!

We were humbled at the goodness of God and the wonderful response of the television audience. Several times while we were doing the broadcast, Marcus said, "The phone lines are jamming. People are calling and asking for prayer."

At the close of the program, we had the opportunity to pray for the requests that had come in via emails, the Web, or telephone calls. Joni and the Daystar singers chose her inspiring song, "This Is Your Moment," as their last song. Months prior to the television interview, she had given me permission to use the song during our praise and worship time when more than 1,200 women came to the South Carolina Women's Retreat to have their "moment" with God, which was based on Joni's song. It was wonderful to hear her perform it *live*.

As Marcus handed me the stack of blue paper the requests were recorded on, my heart was overwhelmed. After my husband preached, we prayed in one accord for those requests, believing for a miracle in the lives of individuals around the world. We heard from many of the viewers in the days that followed.

After the telecast ended, our cell phones lit up with Twitter and Facebook notifications. I almost cried at the outpouring of love we received from those who had watched. Again, I was so humbled.

I'm grateful for the ability to connect with individuals around the world through social media. Along with our appearance with Marcus and Joni, we had an interview with the next generation of hosts, Jonathan and Suzy Lamb in *The Green Room*, which was placed on YouTube. This opened up more ways for hurting people to hear the faithfulness of God and possibly give them hope and receive encouragement. How privileged we are to have these avenues of mass communication.

We enjoyed some personal time with Marcus and Joni afterward. You never know where life will take you. Some forty years ago, Marcus and I attended church together in

Macon, Georgia. We even sang in a small ensemble called the Young Disciples that also included his brother, Gary, and my best friend Kathy Barger.

In recent years, some titles in the church have been changed to include the word *discipleship*. Serving as secretary general for the Church of God, my husband's portfolio includes the Discipleship Division. I'm impressed that even back then as teens, we thought it important to use *disciple*. After all, that's what it is all about, right?

Also, serving in Joni's home state was doubly wonderful. Anytime we were at the same events, the South Carolina ladies always gave her a big shout-out. To be able to connect with old and new friends and be used of God to bless His people—well, there are just no words to express the joy I felt.

Praise Music

Praise and worship music has been another thing that has ministered to me and become an important part of my life. Most of the words are taken from Scripture, and when the Word goes forth, it doesn't return void. You don't even realize the Word penetrating your very being. Psalm 3:3 says, "But thou, O Lord, art a shield for me; my glory, and the lifter up of mine head" (KJV). This verse reminds me of *who* He is. There's nothing quite like getting caught-up in anointed worship, because it turns the attention away from things that affect me and focuses on the One who can handle any problem I am facing. I praise Him for what He's done and I worship Him for who He is. Isaiah 57 talks about the High and Exalted One (see v. 15). What better way to describe our loving Lord.

One of the young people from church gave me a CD of Israel and New Breed. What an inspiration it has been to me through the years. After falling in love with praise music, I've added many more artists whose songs minister to me. I thank God for them all.

Bountiful Blessings

My parents came to Ohio to be with us during the dark time of Summer's illness, and what a blessing it was. They stayed at our house and made sure everything ran smoothly while we were at the hospital. Matthew certainly enjoyed having them as well. They were able to be with us for our state camp meeting, which was a first. It was such a special time for me and a source of real comfort.

A SUMMER STORY
OF GOD'S ENDURING GRACE

Sometimes, blessings are wrapped in unexpected packages. During this time Summer's Persian cat, Sassy, was at a total loss as to what was going on. He was her best buddy ever! Yes, his name was *Sassy* and he was a boy, but since we had watched the movie *Homeward Bound* just before getting him, no other name would do for Summer. We made it better for him by adding *Boy* to his name.

It's so amazing how pets can become part of your life. My mom told us that every day around 3 p.m. when it was time for the school bus to drop Summer off, Sassy would come down the stairs. Having not seen her all day, he would wait for Summer to come in. But she never did. Mom said it was so pitiful to see him just sitting there and looking confused.

Some people say they are just animals, but if you have ever had a pet, you know differently. The pet becomes part of your family. In our case, Sassy was a blessing. I couldn't write Summer's story without including Sassy. We had him for sixteen years, and he moved around the country with us to five different states. It was all Summer ever knew. While she took her bath, he would perch himself right by the tub. When she was sick, he would lie across her stomach; when she went to bed, he would go with her. Many times I would find him on her pillow just like he owned the spot. I would move him for fear he might suffocate her with all his fur. He's been gone for three years now, and she still talks about him like it was yesterday.

CELEBRATIONS!

Youth Camp

Summer got to attend youth camp in Northern Ohio—and, yes, I was a camper too! The workers said, "We've never had an overseer's wife as a camper!" I went to the flag pole every morning just like everyone else. Summer had a wonderful counselor, Shellie Wimmer (Hensley). She would give me time for myself during "fun time." That was awesome!

We had a grand time that week, and it brought back so many memories of when I attended Georgia Youth Camp. That was always the highlight of my summer. I'm so proud the tradition continues to our future generations, because it absolutely changes lives.

I could tell that Shellie was a special young woman. Summer and I were so blessed to have the opportunity to spend the week with her at camp. Now, Shellie is married with children of her own. I am still connected with her via Facebook. She told me that out of all the camps she's been to, the one with Summer holds the best memories.

Challenger Baseball

In the midst of so many setbacks, while we were in Ohio, we found another program called Challenger Baseball. At the time, it was one of a kind in the nation where kids with special needs get the chance to come together as a team and be cheered on to greatness. Summer was chosen to appear on the evening news. We have a copy of the video where she was part of the groundbreaking ceremony for a new field—one of its kind in the country. The shovel was bigger than she was, but she was so proud to be a part of the event.

Summer was privileged to play baseball for many years. There were always trophies and medals to be won by the teams, and we all became a big family. Of course, she couldn't finish out the season that summer after the hemorrhage, and the other players were so sad. Her coach and many team members visited her in the hospital. This would be the last season she would ever play because there would be more hospital visits.

Happy Birthday

Summer turned sixteen while we were serving at Pathway Press in Cleveland. The employees gave her a "Sweet

Sixteen" birthday party that would make the ones you see on television pale in comparison. She was a princess with a tiara, ribbon, a huge cake, and a table full of presents. There were close to one hundred people in attendance as everyone sang, "Happy Birthday." Her eyes were so big they twinkled, filled with excitement. Those moments will be sealed forever in our memories.

Wedding Bells

In the summer of 2006, we moved to Greenville, South Carolina. The next summer was the wedding of our son, Matthew, and his stunning bride, Jennifer. It was a joyous occasion and took place on a beautiful day in Cleveland, Tennessee. Matthew had recently graduated from Lee University; Jennifer had graduated earlier and remained in the area to work. We were all so happy, yet inside I was torn. Summer had a terrible ear infection which required a trip to the doctor. The infection was so bad that without cotton placed in her ear, the drainage would drip down the side of her face into her hair. Then it became a crusty mess. It was the most severe ear infection I could remember, and, of course, it was during the wedding of our son. This would be the only chance for me to be mother of the groom; or, for that matter, mother of a bride.

Also, my mother would not really be able to attend because of crippling arthritis, but she was determined to be at the wedding of her grandson, so my daddy made sure she was there. I wanted to help her enjoy the wedding. She had to use a wheelchair, but we decorated it and made it look festive. Little did we know that this would be the last time Matthew and Jennifer would ever see her this side of heaven. Less than two months later, she was spending her days on the *streets of gold.*

Even with emotions stirring inside, I was so happy for my son. Jennifer was such a gracious bride. She included Summer as a junior bridesmaid with a matching dress just like the big girls. We never intended for her to be in the wedding party due to seizure alert, but I was determined for her to look pretty for the photos. Her ear infection and severe dizziness created more complications, but Jenn made sure she was included. I love her.

After the ceremony, the caregiver took Summer to McDonalds so I could enjoy the reception. Summer thought that was a special treat. *Who would want to stay and eat the finest wedding hors d'oeuvres when you can go to McDonalds?* Doesn't take much to make her happy . . . sometimes.

CELEBRATIONS!

We had one slight problem—how to get all the wedding gifts back to Matthew and Jennifer's new home in South Carolina. Since we already had a car filled with boxes, friends stepped in again. This time it would be Kim and Eddie Allen and Terry and Tony Padgett. The two couples had traveled together and didn't have much room with their luggage, but they made it work. On the trip home, their car broke down somewhere along I-85.

The car was towed so they could get it fixed and be on their way home. It wouldn't do for Kim to leave the gifts in the car while the mechanic tried to assess the problem, so she asked the place of business for extra trash bags and in the gifts went. They sat on the sidelines as hours passed. There they were . . . four people with trash bags sitting all around them. I'm not sure what people must have thought, but they didn't seem to worry about it. After finding out the car was not going to be ready for several days, Roger Childers came from Greenville and picked them up. They were all tired to the point of being silly. I was told it was a fun and fast ride home in the middle of the night, with luggage and gifts in tow. When Matthew and Jennifer arrived home, their gifts were all laid out for them and looking beautiful—except for a couple of mashed bows.

A SUMMER STORY
OF GOD'S ENDURING GRACE

Another High School Graduate

For the most part, going to school was a lot of fun for Summer. Because of her disability, the bus would come right to the end of our driveway in the various places we lived. She loved her friends and could hardly wait to see them each day. She would participate in all the school programs. One day Summer was telling us about a friend and she said, "Her name is Grace."

"That is such a pretty name," I said. "What color is she?"

"Gray," Summer said. She was six years old at the time, and I thought her reply was so "Summer." She was so cute but very serious when describing her new Asian friend.

I would always go on the school field trips with her class. Having Mom around made it better, and an extra adult came in handy for other members of the class. Summer participated in Special Olympics, which was always inspiring to see these athletes win medals.

As time went on, the high school schedule became more structured and the days became long. With the anticipation of seizures, sometimes panic and anxiety would ensue, which meant a trip to the school for early pickup.

Finally, Summer's graduation day came! I think we were all relieved. We celebrated privately because there didn't need to be another occasion for her to receive gifts. She has been so blessed to have many loving people who seem to find joy in giving her so much! Many times we share with underprivileged children, and she's so proud of that fact. Then sometimes she gets a gift and asks, "Do I have to give it to the poor kids?" My six-year-old returns.

Camp Spearhead

Camp Spearhead is a program that has provided thousands of special-needs children and adults with a traditional residential camp experience since 1968. They are based on the belief that everyone deserves a chance to go to camp. Held at the beautiful Pleasant Ridge Camp and Retreat Center located in the foothills of South Carolina's Blue Ridge Mountains, Camp Spearhead serves as a respite to family members while the kids experience freedom, build friendships, and have tons of fun all in an atmosphere of acceptance and love.

We were excited that Summer was able to attend one weekend, knowing she would be well taken care of with a twenty-four-hour medical supervision and wonderfully trained counselors, not to mention that we had a free weekend. But when I thought about her sleeping in a sleeping bag and not being used to it, plus going to a Furman

University football game in the heat of the day, my heart was gripped with fear. Sunday afternoon couldn't come soon enough. I arrived two hours early but didn't want to seem overzealous, so I found a Dunkin Donuts shop in the area and waited. Yes, I had a doughnut.

My fears subsided the moment I arrived and found a very happy Summer. She had a wonderful weekend and a great experience. Even through my distress, I was so happy for her and kind of proud of myself.

Moments of Refreshment

After Mom's death, my dad found another wonderful lady to share his life with. I've known her my entire life and I called her Joyce. Now I call her *Mimi*. I'm so glad my dad isn't alone.

To conclude this chapter, I would like to stop and give thanks for special gifts God has graciously designed to lift my spirits and bring much-needed beauty, joy, and delight to me throughout my life: *Lord, today and every day, I'm thankful for . . .*

- Opportunities to be interviewed on TV and testify of Your faithfulness

CELEBRATIONS!

- Occasions to celebrate
- Faithful friends who lend a listening ear
- Strength and wisdom to care for a sick child
- Loving parents who sacrifice their time
- Pets that brighten the darkest day
- Helpful hands in times of difficulty
- Arms that wrap around me when I need a hug
- Times of humor to lighten the moment.

Proverbs 27:9 reminds us, "Perfume and incense bring joy to the heart, and the pleasantness of one's friend springs from [her] earnest counsel." Think about your own blessings, and take a moment to thank God for each friend and family member who has added a unique "scent" to the perfume of your life.

SUMMER AND HER BUDDY SASSY BOY

YOUTH CAMP, NORTHERN OHIO

JENNIFER AND SUMMER

CHALLENGER
BASEBALL

CHAPTER EIGHT

Be joyful in hope, patient in affliction, faithful in prayer.

—Romans 12:12

LAUGHTER AND TEARS

Laughter is a gift that can be used even in the midst of serious and painful situations. The healing touch of laughter is one of the graces God designed to help us make it through the long dreary hours, days, months, and years of praying for and taking care of a sick child. Laughter will not stop the pain or cure the illness, but when we least expect it, chuckling at ourselves will provide moments of relief that help us bear the pain.

Summer has quite a colorful personality. A bird decided to build its nest outside her window, and it was always singing and chirping. It would awaken her during the night and early mornings, and she became afraid of all birds and didn't want any part of them—not even the fake ones. I learned to use only solid sheets on her bed because if there was a design, she would wake up at night and cry out, "A bug, Mama . . . a bug!" I think she was trying to say *bird*.

On many occasions I would sing at church; and if the song was too slow, Summer would begin to cry, and whoever had her would have to leave the service. It was only when I sang—that could give you a complex.

I had several babysitters who became like family. When we arrived in Hinesville, Georgia, we found a little eleven-year-old girl named Heather Wyatt (Smith), who became like our own daughter. Her mom, Anita, was a dear friend and our church clerk. We would buy groceries together every Saturday and load the car down. I would have $20 worth of vanilla pudding in my buggy. We were so hungry that sometimes we would make a sandwich in the car on the way home. Those were such good times.

My other neighbor was Anne Wright, and she was everyone's Nana. They were good to this young couple who came to be their pastor. Deb (Anne's daughter) and Heather followed in my footsteps and became registered dental hygienists. That is the ultimate compliment. I am so proud of them.

The 'Hound Dog' Incident

Shortly after our move to South Carolina, we had a Christmas party for retired ministers and widows which was held in Columbia. Summer had to go to events if I went, because we didn't have any sitters at the time. She loved listening to her CD; one of her favorites was Elvis Presley, so she usually entertained herself pretty well.

At this particular event, they had a special place for us at the head table. We were doing great. Then they ushered in one of the state councilmen and his seat was right next to Summer. I was hoping she would be a good girl since we hadn't been in South Carolina for very long. We needed to make a good impression.

All was going well . . . until Summer decided she was going to sing along with her CD out loud to Pastor Al Sims. Her singing went something like this: "They said you were high class, but that was just a lie."

Then, of all things, she sang the next line, which was a repeat of the first: "Yes, they said you were high class, but that was just a lie." She kind of mumbled over the next words but ended by saying, "And you ain't no friend of mine."

I was humiliated. Thankfully, Al Sims is such a good man, with a great sense of humor. He became one of her best pals, and we talked and laughed about the incident for many years to come. I still would have felt better if the song could have been "Love Me Tender" or something else besides "Hound Dog."

Special Memories

Summer sometimes knows right from wrong. Daily she will tell me, "*Hate* is a strong word." One time—out of the clear blue—she told Matthew, "Matthew, I don't hate you." But then she said, "Well, I kinda do." Just when we think she has it straight, we find out differently. If I was on Facebook, this is where I would have to say, "LOL!"

When Summer first learned to talk, for some reason, she loved to call herself *Munchie* (pronounced *Muh-chee*). We would say, "You're Summer," and she would say, "No, I *Muh-chee!*" We would repeat it just to get her to argue with us. It was so cute. I have no idea where she got that particular name, but we enjoyed bantering with her. And sometimes she gets names mixed up. She always called the Eddie Allen family, the "Eddies" instead of the Allens. She also has a real connection to our friend Tommy Powell, but to her, his name is "Tommy Powers," as if it were one word. These names stick and we refer to them in the same manner. Another friend, Kip Box, gave her a Webkinz Pink Hearts Love Frog and she named it *Kippy*. I have to be careful not to call him that when we see him.

When we go to churches or doctors' offices, Summer likes to gather up some giveaway things too! She will end up with all kinds of things to take home. One time we were out with one of our pastors and, before we went home, the pastor's wife was emptying her purse so she could give it to Summer. I try to explain to Summer that it's not polite to ask for things, so now she sends everyone to tell me, "She didn't ask for this." It's hopeless!

Dana's Wedding

Dana Dietz is someone who is loved by everyone, and, of course, we are no exception. Several times when we had to go out of town, Dana stayed with Matthew and Summer. She also assisted with the youth group at the local church we attended in Northern Ohio. That was the greatest group of teens. They had so much fun, but they also loved to worship God. Even though they have gone their separate ways, gotten married, and some have babies now, they have stayed in touch and remained friends.

When Dana and Daryl Harmon got engaged, we were excited for them—especially when Dana asked Summer to be one of her flower girls. This was after the stroke, but before the seizures, so Summer was able to participate. She was so cute and thrilled to be part of such a blessed wedding. The Harmons now have two sons of their own.

I will always remember and cherish this memory (this time with tears of joy) because it was one of the few times in her life when Summer got to do the things "normal" little girls do.

The Voices of Lee

The Voices of Lee, under the direction of Danny Murray, is a sixteen-member a capella ensemble from Lee University, Cleveland, Tennessee. For the past nineteen years, they have entertained audiences worldwide with inspirational a capella music. Thrust into the national spotlight on NBC's *Sing-Off* competition in 2009, their second runner-up finish brought them to the attention of thousands of new fans.

We became acquainted with Danny during our Lee days. His joyful personality and excellent musical skills are evident in every aspect of his career. The first time we heard Voices of Lee sing, we fell in love with them. Anytime we get to be at the same event, it is such a highlight for us. During our time at Pathway Press, I remember hearing that they were going to be at the North Chattanooga Church of God where some of our friends, Jim and Kathy Milligan, serve as pastor. After the service that morning, we were asked to go to lunch with all the guests.

Voices of Lee travel the country in a big, beautiful tour bus. When Summer saw it, she asked if she could ride with them to the restaurant, and, of course, Danny said, "Yes, be my guest," which meant I had to hop aboard, too. Summer rode in the front captain's seat with Debbie, Danny's wife. That was a thrilling day for Summer!

While we were serving in South Carolina, Voices were the special guests for us during our state camp meeting for several consecutive years. They did the annual state women's luncheon, as well as the youth night service. The group is always well received on- and off-stage. They are an amazingly talented group of students who obviously love the Lord.

Through the years, the group changes members due to graduation and new students added, but the sound and spirit remains the same. Recently, when my husband preached at the Michigan Church of God Camp Meeting, Voices heard a portion of Summer's testimony. As I write tonight, I just found out that each night during their devotion, they call Summer's name in prayer. Once again, I am overwhelmed by God's grace and the goodness of His people. I am so blessed to know this incredible group of university students!

Blessings and Gifts

Through the years, the special people we have worked with have always made Summer's birthday and Christmas extremely exciting. Of course, arriving to a new place and then departing was no different.

As we were moving to South Carolina, we were asked, "Do we need to build a wheelchair ramp?" That melted my heart. They didn't know exactly what was wrong, but they were preparing the way to make it easy for us. And then as we left to move back to Tennessee, again they blessed us with gifts, but always made sure Summer was not forgotten. I've already mentioned the 24-inch Miami Sun trike they gave her, but there were also many more gifts.

It had been a tiring week of packing boxes, but a reception had been planned to say our farewells. The leadership and office staff are incredible, as well as the pastors and laity, and it was going to be an emotional evening. Summer was *feeling* a seizure (aura) and anxiety was rising. I wanted her to be able to participate and say goodbye, but I didn't want the last vision they had of her to be having a seizure. Most of them had never seen that. It can be devastating. So I called her caregiver to come and pick her up. Everyone was always so understanding.

What do you do without people to help you through life? I don't know. How do you ever repay them? You don't;

you can't. Saying *thank you* seems so trite. I can only ask God to give back to them in the same measure they have given to us—pressed down, shaken together, and running over (see Luke 6:38)!

Locked Outside

One day I was locked outside in the detached garage at our house. Summer had already gone inside the house alone. But when I went to open the door, it wouldn't open. I tried to find tools to remove the doorknob but to no avail. I lifted the window, and even though it was a little far to jump, I was going to risk it. I tried to remove the screen but couldn't. I had my phone, but I didn't have any of my neighbors' numbers or complete names to call 411; so, before I called 911 or destroyed property, I called my husband, who was thirty minutes away. While he was en route, he called a neighbor to see if they could come over and open the door.

Prior to my neighbor getting there, Summer came out looking for me, and I said through the window, "Come here and open the door."

She turned quickly and went back inside. I thought maybe she was going to get a jacket or put on some different shoes. She was probably wondering why I hadn't come in, but she didn't come back. My neighbor finally arrived and tried the door, but it wouldn't open from the outside either.

I told her it was OK, my husband was on the way. I was concerned about Summer, so I thought maybe if I call the house, she would answer, because that's what we do when we're out of town. I called several times, and she finally came back outside and yelled, "The phone keeps ringing!"

I said, "It's me." So, instead of coming and talking to me through the window or checking on me, she goes back inside so I could call again and talk to her on the phone. I asked her, "Why didn't you come and help me?"

"I thought you were a stranger," she said. You have to love how these kids think! Finally, my "knight in shining armor," brandishing an ax, rescued me! It only cost a replacement doorknob and all was well again at the Propes' home.

A TYPICAL "SUMMER" DAY

Although Summer has been beaten up by life with pain, surgery, and years of fighting just to survive, all the wonder and innocence of childhood are still in place—even the monitor that most parents use for small infants. Her day is normally filled with lots of talking and chattering! She loves to watch her morning programs on television, but as she continues to watch throughout the day, she still calls them her "morning programs."

When the weather is nice, she loves to splash around in the swimming pool, or ride her bike. Both activities are so wonderful because of the sunshine (vitamin D) and exercise she is getting while being outside.

Bon Appetite

Summer loves to eat—anything! Just one thing doesn't work; she loves a variety of foods, which makes it easy to prepare her a balanced meal. She likes a snack while I'm preparing her breakfast, so I lay out some grapes and green tea. Before taking a bite, she always counts the grapes. No matter how many grapes I give her, fifteen magically appear.

Don't think a bowl of cereal is sufficient! It's just not exciting enough, I guess. She goes to bed early, so she will be rising early in the morning. Around 8 a.m. she is getting her breakfast stuff out, which consists of eggs (or egg beaters) and "anything but the kitchen sink" veggies to go into an omelet with grits and toast. We have ventured out to have some different options on mornings when we need to spend less time in the kitchen and do other things.

When we lived in South Carolina, one of her state-provided benefits was to receive Mom's Meals, which consisted of fourteen, fresh-made, home-delivered meals, with all the trimmings, every two weeks. What a blessing . . . and they were delicious. She enjoyed picking out the one she wanted to eat. It sure made my life simpler. We don't have those anymore and I really miss them.

Summer loves games. Sometimes she and I play "pretend." She loves for me to pretend I'm her waitress and she orders her food. My cousin played that game with me when I was a little girl, and I will always remember the great relationship we shared. The difference with my childhood game and with Summer today is that I got to actually order from a menu my cousin had made out. Summer already knows what she is going to have; I just have to go to her "table" and take her order. She loves to eat so much that as soon as we finish eating, immediately she starts planning the next meal. When she and I are alone, her go-to lunch is a sandwich and soup. She loves to pick the soup, though, so I keep a good variety in the pantry. We should have bought stock in Crystal Light Peach tea, because this girl can drink a lot of tea!

The caregivers follow the same routine, for the most part. Summer requires certain things from differet caregivers, and she keeps us all straight.

A "Summer" Day Continues

After we finish with breakfast and the details of clean-up, Summer likes to pick out her clothes for the day. She has become very good at selecting things that match with the same colors. The top may be stripes and the bottom plaid. (They go together now, right?) Most days she looks like Pippi Longstocking, the fictional children's book character, but it's OK, as long as we don't have plans to go anywhere.

If you walked into Summer's bedroom, you would be greeted by all her stuffed animals, which are her constant companions. She has given each one a special name. They play games with her, and she always congratulates them if they win. If she forgets to congratulate them, she will apologize and say, "I think I need to go to 'timeout.'"

And I say, "OK."

Then she asks, "How long should I stay?"

"About five minutes," I respond, which ends up being about thirty seconds.

Several of her stuffed animals sit with her at mealtime, go to the mall with her, and, of course, attend church with her.

Since she is still in the Disney phase, I am very thankful for the Disney Channel. She likes everything except *Jake and the Never Land Pirates*. I don't think she likes Captain Hook, so when he appears, we usually change the channel to Nickelodeon.

Summer loves for me to read to her. I don't have to read much because—after her meds, brushing her teeth, and putting lotion on her face, along with our nighttime routine—she is ready to go to sleep. Her favorite book is a personalized Disney's *Winnie the Pooh*. She loves it because it mentions her name and the names of her friends.

Remembering Jesus

All of Matthew's and Summer's lives, we have made Communion part of our worship at church as well as at home. So, partaking of the Lord's Supper is very familiar to Summer. She thinks Jesus has great snacks (Communion). We've tried to explain Communion in a very simplistic way because she would be very concerned about His blood and broken body, so we tell her, "It is the way we remember Jesus." Some people may think she shouldn't take Communion because she doesn't fully understand, but she probably understands more than we know. And besides, she spots the prepared Communion cup when we sit down, so for her not to participate would be nothing short of a meltdown. I'm so glad Jesus sees our heart and understands everything about us.

The Waiting Room

While we were serving in South Carolina, I wrote an article for my newsletter that was mailed quarterly to the pastors' wives, giving an update on Summer, including some photos of her. When Summer saw it, she wanted a copy of it. That was a couple of years ago.

Recently, Summer and I were at a doctor's office, and the receptionist called me back to the window to take care of some insurance matters. When I turned around to check on Summer, she had given the article to a woman to read. I was amazed and surprised for a couple of reasons: First, I didn't realize Summer still had the article in her purse; and, second, I couldn't believe she had the forethought to give it to someone to read. She usually depends on me to explain her medical history to people, but I guess she figured I was busy and she handled it the best way she knew how.

Summer's new acquaintance said, "This is so encouraging." I could tell she was really enjoying talking to Summer and reading about her. Obviously, I didn't know how the article would be received by a stranger, but when I looked over at the person who was with her, I noticed that she was sitting in a wheelchair and wearing a T-shirt that said, "Jesus is my BFF!" I knew then we were in good company.

My Hectic Schedule

As hard as we try to have a regular routine, there are those days that are filled with anxiety and unexpected turns. When it's time for me to give her the different daily medicines, my heart goes out to her because she will hold out her little trembling hand, but she takes whatever I give her with no questions, whether it is a Tylenol or a cup full of medicine. Such blind faith!

Each day is filled with new surprises, and we always have the possibility of a seizure and the anticipation of more to come. The anxiety of that anticipation clouds her day; however, we have learned to live with whatever happens. Sometimes the seizure passes, sometimes it doesn't. We remember the funny times because it helps to take us through the not-so-funny times. With the Lord's help, we make it one day at a time.

Like most of you, I have several electronic devices for quick access to my friends and the cyber world, but I don't think I will ever be completely paperless. I must keep one calendar for a particular medicine for Summer, a separate calendar for her seizure activity during the day, and then a calendar with my schedule on it. Sometimes the days are too short. I feel like I'm constantly journaling and juggling the things on my "plate." Recently I read where journaling is like a farmer tilling the soil—only this is my life that is being tilled. When I take time to jot down my feelings and current dilemmas, it is incredible to see the way feelings slip out the end of my pen with solutions to problems I did not know were possible.

As I'm writing tonight, she has just had a seizure and has not been able to keep any food down for about twenty-four hours, except for Sprite and a few crackers. These are the dark times, the days when we hold on, believing God for our family and praying for a new day. It always comes. And with that new day comes new hope and the determination to keep striving for all that God has for us. It's amazing what a good night's rest will do for a tired body and mind. I used to tell Matthew, "Things will be better in the morning."

DANA'S WEDDING

CHAPTER NINE

*It's useless to rise early
and go to bed late, and work
your worried fingers to the bone.
Don't you know he [God] enjoys
giving rest to those he loves?*

—Psalm 127:2 TM

STAYING FOCUSED

CARING FOR A CHILD WHO HAS SPECIAL NEEDS REQUIRES round-the-clock focus, which can lead to exhaustion. I've learned that the biggest hindrance to staying focused is excessive busyness, continuous stress, and lack of rest. And rest is more than just sleep. Rest calms, soothes, and refreshes. Jesus said, "Come with me by yourselves to a quiet place and get some rest" (Mark 6:31).

One of the things that has helped me is not to just focus on having a *quantity* of rest but a *quality* of rest. Sometimes I take five or ten minutes in the middle of my harried schedule to clear out the debris of worry and focus on God's Word. A scripture that gives me peace is Philippians 4:8-9: "Whatever is true, whatever is noble, whatever is right, whatever is pure, whatever is lovely, whatever is admirable—if anything is excellent or praiseworthy—think about such things. Whatever you have learned or received or heard from me, or seen in me—put it into practice. And the God of peace will be with you."

A website I found on the Internet lists the following health benefits of rest:

- Improved memory
- Improved creativity and work performance
- Greater ability to concentrate and focus
- Greater ability to maintain a healthy weight
- Greater ability to manage stress
- Greater ability to avoid accidents

(*Health.com*)

This website also has exercises, dieting tips, and other healthy habits to increase your stamina and rid your day of happiness-robbers.

Superhighway of Duties

Do you feel there is not enough time in one day to get your "to-do list" finished before it's time to start over again? I do. And the Bible warns us not to grow weary in well doing. But day after day, year after year, the care we give, the doctors' appointments, and the disappointments we live with can wear us down. God knew we would become discouraged, so we need to remember . . . "in due season we shall reap, if we faint not" (Gal. 6:9 KJV). The NIV translates verses 9 and 10 this way: "Let us not become weary in doing good, for at the proper time we will reap a harvest if we do not give up. Therefore, as we have opportunity, let us do good to all people, especially to those who belong to the family of believers."

You are not reading this book by accident. I have been praying for you a long time. I know your pain; I understand your doubts; and I've lived with long-term care of a loved one. So, don't give up! You will make it . . . by God's grace. And, I will too!

Spare Time (Really?!)

Although I haven't always had the privilege (or the time) to keep an ongoing journal, I think it is so important to jot down things of concern—especially when I can see God's hand moving in mine and Summer's lives. When inspiration strikes, and because time is of the essence, I have to use what is handy, which may be a single piece of paper. But nonetheless, I make it work and try not to miss anything. I usually keep these thoughts in one place so I can read them again. I know the day will come when I will need them.

It is amazing for me to relive events of a day and see how the ups and downs, the uncertainties, the timeless routines keep the "wheel of doing good" rolling. We must keep pressing on.

Summer and I also watch a lot of the old family classics together—over and over. One of my favorites is *Angels in the Outfield*, yet another baseball picture. You've seen movies like this where the plot is obvious. You know all great home runs happen when the batter is facing a 3-2 count, that all crucial pitches must be in slow motion, and that, no matter how many of these films they make, Hollywood will never feel the genre has been exhausted. I don't guess I will either.

To this day, I get teary-eyed when all ends well. In this particular movie, I especially love the repetition of the phrase "It could happen." Not only do I have the feel-good emotion of another great movie (albeit cheesy), but I'm also reminded of God's Word: "With God all things are possible" (Matt. 19:26)! Nothing you or I will ever face is too difficult for Him. Once again, I am comforted knowing that He knows my needs.

I remember a "thus-saith-the-Lord" word spoken during a state meeting we attended long ago in South Georgia: "What is over your head is under My feet." These words have gone with me through every situation I face in life, reminding me that when I feel like I am drowning, He is walking on top of the situation!

Friends Who Brighten the Day

While attending a Sonfest in Orlando, Florida, my friend Pam Taylor and I went shopping. Summer has always loved *Goofy*, the funny animal cartoon character created at Walt Disney Productions. Goofy is a tall, anthropomorphic dog that wears a turtleneck sweater and vest, with pants, shoes, white gloves, and a tall, rumpled fedora. He is a close friend of Mickey Mouse and Donald Duck, and is one of Disney's most popular characters. Summer had her heart set on having her own Goofy, but all I could find was a seasonal one. He was not dressed like the one we had seen on Disney's cartoons. But since we didn't have a lot of time to shop, I said, "This will be fine; she won't know the difference." So I bought it. We left and didn't think about it again.

Two weeks later, Summer received a large package in the mail with a card that read: "This is the *real* Goofy, just for you." This thoughtful gesture brought tears to my eyes.

Pam would not be satisfied with the imitation; she wanted Summer to have the authentic Goofy.

Recently, Pam and I had lunch, and before I left, she handed me another stuffed animal for Summer. She never forgets her.

The Power of Music

Music can be another incredible source of inspiration and motivation in staying focused. It's almost like a waste not to make use of it! According to the American Music Therapy Association, music is restorative for a wide variety of conditions, even aiding those with physical rehabilitation and assisting those with disabilities. Music therapy can ease the pains of chemotherapy, lower anxiety, lift a depressed person's spirit, and help insomniacs go to sleep. Music is unable to cure cancer or chronic disease, but it can relieve aches and symptoms while augmenting a patient's joy and general well-being.

Although I do not know the situation Andrae Crouch was addressing when he wrote the beloved song, "Through It All," I do know those words have struck a chord of familiarity to probably millions of Christians who have had tears and sorrow of various kinds. The powerful line in the song declares: "I've learned to depend upon His Word." This is the hidden secret that unfolds in every trial—learning to depend on God's unfailing Word.

Your favorite song can be not only a great motivator but also a vehicle to elicit positive emotions within you, stirring a spirit of optimism. If the songs are chosen wisely, the music will energize you and get you into that classic I-can-do-anything mind-set.

When Matthew was young, he used to enjoy having me sing to him. Sometimes he would join in, but Summer didn't like that so much. If the song was too slow, or if the lyrics were what she perceived as sad, she would hurry through the song and want to sing something peppier. She loves to create her own tunes by making them up as she goes. They are really catchy tunes, too.

This is one she sings to the tune of the "ABC Song": "I love Jesus; I love God. I hate the devil, yes I do." At times I get one of those tunes stuck in my mind and it's a little frustrating. She also really enjoys listening to CDs. One time I saw an educational program advertising a CD that had been proven to be very soothing for special-needs children, especially during anxious moments. The CD is by Nolwenn Leroy, a French singer and songwriter, and the entire tape is in French. I thought I would try it since Summer loves to listen. Her favorite song was "Cassé," which was the first song on the CD, so we heard it a lot. On the chorus, Summer always thought it said *Got saved* instead of *Cassé*. So she would sing, "Got saved (*Cassé*)! Oh, oh, got saved (*Cassé*)!" and she would just sing her little heart out. The word *cassé* translates into English as "broken," so I guess that was a good substitution.

Before I tuck her in for the night, we pray together. This is Summer's bedtime prayer:

> *I love You, Jesus; I love You, God.*
> *God, don't let me feel a seizure tonight.*
> *Don't let me have a seizure tonight.*
> *Heal me.*
> *Heal Rachel and Katie, God; don't let them be crippled.*
> *Amen!*

(Rachel and Katie are twins who used to live across the street from us and have cerebral palsy.)

Refueling Our Energy

Because life is full of unpleasant surprises and setbacks, I think it's important to get a dose of inspiration and encouragement to refuel our energy. In Ephesians 5:19-20, the apostle Paul suggested encouraging himself and other Christians in corporate worship through song: "Speak to one another with psalms, hymns and spiritual songs. Sing and make music in your heart to the Lord, always giving thanks to God the Father for everything, in the name of our Lord Jesus Christ."

Also, I enjoy listening to motivational CDs, hearing scriptures read aloud, reading encouraging books by many different authors, and masterminding with like-minded individuals. These inspiring habits help me to develop what I call *mental toughness*—something we all need at different times in our lives.

Over the years in ministry, we've had access to many resources and received many books and products. Being the inquisitive person that I am, I read them before I put them away—I don't want to miss a thing. I've always believed there may be something within those pages or in a line of a particular song that will carry me through a tough spot—and I've always been right. And if you're part of my family, I want you to hear it too.

While we lived in Ohio, we had Dr. Bryan Cutshall, pastor of Twin Rivers Worship Center in Saint Louis, Missouri, for a state meeting, and he shared some of his ministry products with us. Of course, I read them and thought our son, Matthew, needed to do so as well. Since his reading might get lost in schoolwork or extracurricular activities, I read to him aloud as he drove us to church. I had a captive audience for about forty minutes three times a week. Thankfully, he was a great listener and didn't seem to mind. It made me feel better, too.

Listening for God's Voice

When we face life's obstacles and challenges, we will need extra motivation, full commitment, total determination, extra drive, patience, and persistence to overcome them. I can always go to God's Word and find how He talked loudly and directly to people (like Moses, Aaron, Miriam, Noah, Abraham, and all the prophets). Sometimes He used words, but most of the time He communicated through visions and dreams.

In the New Testament, God spoke to Elizabeth and Zacharias, Mary and Joseph, and to Paul on the Damascus road. Also, through a vision, God spoke the Book of Revelation to John on the isle of Patmos. He still speaks today, but it seems most often He speaks through His Word and in a small voice—even a whisper. When we face challenges that seem too hard to conquer, we seek His guidance. Our obedience turns up the volume and enables us to hear the "still, small voice" (see 1 Kings 19:12). The more we live in His Word and live like Him, the clearer the voice of the Holy Spirit becomes.

Lessons Learned in the Dark

Worry loves darkness. When the last light is dimmed and you settle down to rest, every problem and challenge of the day is magnified. Jennifer Rothchild's book, *Lessons I Learned in the Dark* (*Steps to Walking by Faith, Not by Sight*), offers poignant autobiographical sketches that illuminate a path to freedom and fulfillment despite adversity. At the age of fifteen, Jennifer confronted two unshakable realities: *Blindness is inevitable . . .* and *God is enough.* This popular author, speaker, and recording artist gives the reader a glimpse of her unique—yet universal—struggle of how she has learned to live out her faith in the dark.

Many times the words of others actually have far more impact and insightfulness than when those same words are read within the pages of a book or a magazine. Lessons learned from those in leadership and others in ministry can be easily incorporated into our everyday duties and tasks.

Kelly Wahlquist, a writer and speaker, has a wonderful blog that I stumbled upon which gave me an injection of encouragement to boost my spirits. It was titled "Until God Opens the Next Door, Praise Him in the Hallway," and it really spoke to me when I needed hope. She explains it this way: "Salvation and Church history are riddled with stories of praise and thanksgiving during times of suffering and great trial. Job experienced life at its worst; David faced years of terror running from Saul; and Paul and Silas were beaten and thrown into prison, yet all responded by singing praise to God."

But what if we pray and believe and the window does not open? Do we give up and spiral down to despair? No way! I like the way Kelly explains this dilemma:

> Sometimes that window takes longer to open than we had hoped. It's up to us what we do while we wait. I say, do what you naturally do when you're waiting for something. Grab a good book—actually, grab the best book . . . the Bible, and listen to the words of your Father. Then, simply talk to Him. Put on some good music or sing a song of praise, because 'Our God Is an Awesome God.' And, above all, know that your suffering has meaning, and offer it up for another.

Blessings of Sharing

If you are not familiar with Laura Story's song, "Blessings," you need to search for it on YouTube and listen to the words. She also shares her testimony of her husband's illness and disability and how God has sustained them throughout their marriage.

Often we miss the value of sharing our true feelings and struggles. We don't want to be vulnerable, so we hold back. In doing so, we deprive others of our experience, our learning, and our humanity. Sharing our own experiences, especially our challenges, not only increases empathy, but also makes us more approachable and relatable.

Although we may ask God *when* and *if* our dreams might come true, our present answer may involve waiting and sharing His blessings. God does not deal in deadlines and due dates, but His Word overflows with the reassurance that He is near us no matter what the day, year, or situation brings our way. I love the verse in Isaiah that says, "Do not fear, for I am with you; do not be dismayed, for I am your God. I will strengthen you and help you; I will uphold you with my righteous right hand" (41:10).

God's Word Builds Trust

A surrendered life is all about trust—trusting that God has our best interests at heart and that His Word can be believed and taken at face value. It is trusting that all of our needs will be met. Surrender takes the focus off of self and places it upon Christ.

Pastor Rick Warren of Saddleback Church in Lake Forest, California, writes, "Surrender is not the best way to live; it is the only way to live. Nothing else works. All other approaches lead to frustration, disappointment, and self-destruction."

Reading and memorizing God's Word is a sustainer of trust. I gain strength from reading different versions of the same passage. For example, 2 Corinthians 4:7-12 in the *New Living Translation* speaks to me in everyday language:

> We now have this light shining in our hearts, but we ourselves are like fragile clay jars containing this great treasure. This makes it clear that our great power is from God, not from ourselves. We are pressed on every side by troubles, but we are not crushed. We are perplexed, but not driven to despair. We are hunted down, but never abandoned by God. We get knocked down, but we are not destroyed. Through suffering, our bodies continue to share in the death of Jesus so that the life of Jesus may also be seen in our bodies. Yes, we live under constant danger of death because we serve Jesus, so that

the life of Jesus will be evident in our dying bodies. So we live in the face of death, but this has resulted in eternal life for you.

CHAPTER TEN

*"You can trust the Man who
died for you."*

—Elizabeth Elliot

TRUSTING GOD IN THE FOG

When God is at work in our lives, we may not be able to recognize Him at first, especially when the fog sets in, worry nags at our hearts, and we are confused. But usually if we look closely, we can see the fingerprints of God on our situation. At that point, what is our response? Do we stay in the boat and slowly make our way to shore like the other disciples did when they saw Jesus walking on the water? Or do we dive in headfirst like Peter, rushing to our Lord as fast as we can?

When I read Romans 8:28—"And we know that God causes all things to work together for good to those who love God, to those who are called according to His purpose" (NASB)—I think, *There is no* maybe *in the scripture above.* We know without a shadow of a doubt God causes all things to work together for our good. He works in the bad things, in the unexplainable things, in the things that trouble us. Sometimes we have a hard time understanding this scripture because we don't see the whole picture. We can't see why God is withholding the answer, so we have to go blindly forward in faith, believing that in the end, God will have accomplished the best thing for us.

Test of Faith

This journey with Summer has required blind trust. In David Jeremiah's wonderful book, *A Bend in the Road: Experiencing God When Your World Caves In*, he makes a significant point: "For every pilgrim in this journey of life, the road will bend in a different direction. We can never know in advance which way it will turn, for the map doesn't display that kind of detail for us. We must meet the bend or the dip or the steep, uphill climb that has been set in the path for each of us. And we look to God for the grace to meet that defining moment." This requires trust. Trusting God in the face of disappointment is the ultimate test of faith. Anyone can walk away when life gets tough. Anyone can be a Sunday-morning Christian, but very few know what it takes to survive out on the battlefield.

Someone has said that worry and confusion are tools God uses to strengthen our faith. But they are also God's tools to drive us into His loving arms of trust. At times, it may seem as if nothing is worse than not knowing what's going on or what's going to happen next. I am sure we all have moments when we wish we could hit "fast forward" to see how everything turns out in the end. Unfortunately (or maybe *fortunately*), we can't do that. We have to take things one step at a time, and sometimes in the fog we can't even see the next step we are taking.

If you have been to the mountains, the coastal waters, or crossed the Tennessee River after a hard rain, you have experienced the fog. It is mysterious and can be soothing, almost like a gentle rain. But it can also be very dangerous and elusive and should be handled with extreme caution. The visibility is limited, and anyone driving should take it slow to avoid an accident.

Our spiritual walk is no different. Proverbs 3:5-6 reminds us, "Trust in the Lord with all your heart, and lean not on your own understanding; in all your ways acknowledge Him, and He shall direct your paths" (NKJV). When I saw Summer lying in a coma on that cooling blanket in the NICU at Akron Children's Hospital, with her head completely bandaged, I trusted God. When the doctors told us she had a high fever and a 6 cm. bleed in her brain, I trusted God. When she has severe seizures on a regular basis, I trust God. My husband says, "In times of great difficulty, you can either run *to* God or run *away* from God. We run to Him." This is our test of faith!

We Are Not in Control

God is teaching us to trust Him, and He always comes through. More than anything else in this world, God desires a deep and intimate relationship with His children. That was the purpose of sending Jesus. He will go to great lengths to get our attention. Sometimes the only way He will do this is to prove to us that we cannot accomplish His will for our lives without Him. That's when He has to convince us how much we need Him in order to teach our hearts to truly love Him. The best way to do this is to show us that we are not in control.

As a way of holding on to His words, in my quiet times, I sit down, listen, and write what I hear Him saying deep in my heart. He wants you and me to put our faith in Him, not in answers to the questions that plague us. He wants to make us give everything we have, even when the way is not clear and the outcome is unknown. I think of Summer and how she trusts me completely with her entire being.

She knows I am going to take care of her—no matter what. This is such a reminder of how I should trust my heavenly Father.

Disappointment is never God's fault. It is always our fault for assuming too much and knowing too little. God does not expect us to understand what is going on in our lives; He does promise us abundant life (see John 10:10) and what is best for us in the end. There are things we will never understand, and He will never punish us for not understanding, but there may be consequences if we fail to trust Him and obey His leading.

One of my heroes is Corrie ten Boom, a Holocaust survivor and world-renown speaker. After World War II, Corrie spoke of her imprisonment at Ravensbruck concentration camp. In her book *The Hiding Place*, she shared the story of her war experiences in Holland and how God ministered to her and her sister, Betsy, in prison.

Many times during her address, she would take a piece of cloth with a crown embroidered on it. First, she would hold up the cloth with the lovely embroidered side showing a beautiful crown, which she described as the plan God has for our lives. Then she would flip the cloth over to reveal the tangled, confused underside—illustrating how we view our lives from a human standpoint. Corrie often quoted the following poem:

THE WEAVER

My life is but a weaving
Between my God and me.
I do not choose the colors
He worketh steadily.

Ofttimes He weaveth sorrow
And I in foolish pride
Forget He sees the upper
And I the underside.

Not till the loom is silent
And the shuttles cease to fly
Will God unroll the canvas
And explain the reasons why.

The dark threads are as needful,
In the skillful Weaver's hands
As the threads of gold and silver
In the pattern He has planned.

Variations of this poem are many and almost always credited to "Author Unknown." I did find one version that credited the writing to B. M. Franklin (1882-1965). In the '70s, the poem was put to music by a gospel songwriter. But the message remains the same: We are not in control, and the dark threads are needed to complete God's plan for our lives.

Bridge of Contentment

Contentment is accepting God's sovereign control over all of life's circumstances. Most of us either try too hard or we quit trying at all. In both cases, we miss God. We miss His infusion of strength that leads to contentment. When we learn contentment, we see God in a new way, and we know that He is the One who is the Blessed Controller of all things.

My journey to contentment began early in life. Of course, the *last* time I got saved (I went to the altar many times "just to make sure") was when I was twelve years of age. My mother said she never really saw any difference because I was always the same. I have loved the Lord my entire life, and have taken God at His Word. This is not to say that I haven't ever been anxious, worried, concerned, or afraid. I have always wanted to "fix" things for those I love. But I have found that hiding in the secret place of the Almighty is the best place for me and my loved ones.

Most of us tend to categorize our lives in both positive and negative ways. We could write a glowing list of the positives in our life, and then write a list of sobering negatives. Both lists are true, but the focus of each list is different. Through the years, I have learned the following list of "I will nots" help keep me focused on contentment—even through the fog:

- I will not complain about anything—not even the weather.

- I will not picture myself in any other circumstances or someone else's shoes.

- I will not allow myself to wish this or that had been different.

- I will not compare my lot with someone else.

- I will not dwell on tomorrow because tomorrow is God's, not mine.

The apostle Paul, whose life was filled with anything but positive circumstances, makes an amazing statement in the Book of Philippians:

> I am not saying this because I am in need, for I have learned to be content whatever the circumstances. I know what it is to be in need, and I know what it is to have plenty. I have learned the secret of being content in any and every situation, whether well fed or hungry, whether living in plenty or in want. I can do everything through him who gives me strength (4:11-13).

Remember, the apostle wrote these words while imprisoned in a dark, dreary dungeon without sanitation or heat. While chained to a guard, he must have wondered if all of his work for Christ really mattered, but he still *learned* to be content. Paul's exhortation not to worry or be anxious means that our anxiety should be used as a springboard to pray specifically (v. 6). Our part in the process of learning to be content is a heart choice—a choice to pray rather than be anxious.

Summer's simple prayers reveal a great mount of trust in the One who teaches us the lessons of contentment.

Making the Right Choice

When confronted with negative circumstances, we have a choice: Will we pray about the problem or will we worry about it? In Philippians 4:7 we see God's part in the contentment process: "And the peace of God, which transcends all understanding, will guard your hearts and your minds in Christ Jesus." If we make the choice to pray instead of worry, we will personally experience God's peace. What a promise! In a world of chaos, problems, heartache, and anxiety, who does not need peace?

Martin Luther is credited with saying, "I have held many things in my hands, and I have lost them all; but whatever I have placed in God's hands, that I still possess." When difficult circumstances come into my life, I hear God's voice saying, "LaQuita, let Me be in control; let Me handle the situation. Accept My timing; accept My ways. Make secret choices that will honor Me. Though no one sees your choices or knows how difficult they are, make them for Me."

Keep Walking

This walk of faith (sometimes in the fog) is difficult because we're asked to believe what we cannot see. This means we often have to walk on a dark path. My problem is, I like light better than the dark or the foggy night. If I can see what God is doing—how He is working everything together for good—then I don't need faith. But still I want to see. (This is not my problem alone.) We say we want more faith, but really what we want is sight. Sight says, "I see that it's good for me." God asks us to keep walking, because He is holding our hand.

I'm so glad I didn't know the first thirteen years of Summer's life what would happen on that Memorial Day weekend in 2002. If I had known, I would have been overwhelmed with emotions, to say the least, and I would have been trying my best to find a solution. We cannot live independent on our own knowledge. That is not trusting God. And He asks us to cast our cares on Him because He loves us.

I love the old hymn written in 1904 by Civilla D. Martin. I sang some of the beautiful verses growing up in church. During a time of doubt or discouragement, I still sing this song—reminding me of God's intimate care. Immediately, my faith is renewed and my spirits are lifted.

GOD WILL TAKE CARE OF YOU

Be not dismayed whate'er betide,
God will take care of you;
Beneath His wings of love abide,
God will take care of you.

Refrain

God will take care of you,
Through every day, o'er all the way;
He will take care of you,
God will take care of you.

Through days of toil when heart doth fail,
God will take care of you;
When dangers fierce your path assail,
God will take care of you.

All you may need He will provide,
God will take care of you;
Nothing you ask will be denied,
God will take care of you.

No matter what may be the test,
God will take care of you;
Lean, weary one, upon His breast,
God will take care of you.

When I'm feeling really low and need His assurance, I sing, "God will take care of *me . . .*" (instead of *you*). These words are so inspiring and reassuring that after a few minutes, my spirits are lifted and I know the words I'm singing are true.

More Than Enough

Earlier in chapter 5, my husband wrote about the dark time he went through during (and months after) Summer's stroke. The darkness seemed suffocating. We can't understand what God is doing and, at the time, we can't seem to discover any possible good in the darkness. As I look back over my life, my deepest intimacy with Him has come from the dark times. The lessons He has burned into my heart when the fog and clouds hovered around me are the ones that have developed my trust and faith in His faithfulness.

Has God asked you to trust Him with the illness of a child, a financial crisis, or a time when you couldn't feel His presence? Do you trust in the fact of God's Word or only in what you can see in the light? I invite you to take a look at the foggy shoreline of your life right now. Are you worried about the future and confused about what's going on in your life? Take heart, and look for the One who meets us in the fog. He's there when we cannot see Him; He is there when we cannot hear Him; and He's even there when we cannot feel Him. Even though He doesn't answer all of our questions, He will always reveal who He is—and that is more than enough!

CHAPTER ELEVEN

Be joyful always; praying continually;
give thanks in all circumstances,
for this is God's will for
you in Christ Jesus.

—1 Thessalonians 5:16-18

COUNTING MY BLESSINGS

IF YOU KNOW INDIVIDUALS WHO DO NOT HAVE STRESSFUL and negative things in their lives, I would like to meet them. However, I don't expect to hear my cell phone jammed with calls or my email crammed with responses. It's just not reality. We live in an imperfect world with problems that can become overwhelming, but everyone has reasons also to be thankful.

Becoming more aware of our blessings will jump-start a trail of gratitude that will end in finding life changes—maybe not on the outside but on the inside where it really counts. Appreciating what is right in our lives is a habit well worth forming.

Thankfulness Is a Choice

Henry J. Nouwen said: "Those who keep speaking about the sun while walking under a cloudy sky are messengers of hope, the true saints of our day." God is interested in using you and me as living object lessons to others who need to hear that we have endured hard times and can praise Him anyhow. A whole new dimension is opened up to those who give God thanks for His plan—including the pain.

Deliberately, even in all our hectic schedules, we can stop for a few minutes a day and remember the reasons we have to be grateful. This can take some practice to perfect. When feelings of distress, frustration—even doubt—start to overwhelm us and the burdens of life seem too heavy, we can ask God for an attitude adjustment. The surprising thing about choosing to be grateful is that it shines a spotlight on the many things we have to thank God for.

Matthew Henry, well-known for his *Commentary on the Whole Bible*, consciously practiced living in gratitude. More than 250 years ago, he wrote these words in his diary after he was robbed of all his money:

> First, let me be thankful because I was never robbed before. Second, because although they took my purse, they did not take my life. Third, that although they took my all, it was not much. Fourth, because it was I who was robbed, not I that did the robbing.

Matthew Henry had trained himself so well to live thankfully that even when something dreadful happened to him, such as a personal robbery, he chose to be grateful.

I'm not suggesting we should keep a diary for others to read two centuries from now, but I do know that there is tremendous value in keeping a "gratitude" journal for ourselves, and maybe for our children and grandchildren. I don't often throw pity parties, but if I start to feel a little sorry for myself, fifteen minutes of reading old entries is a sure cure for the blues.

Singing this wonderful old song is another way to calm the nerves and clear out the "cobwebs" of worry and frustration:

When I'm worried and I can't sleep
I count my blessing instead of sheep
And I fall asleep, counting my blessings.

If you're worried and you can't sleep
Just count your blessings instead of sheep
And you'll fall asleep counting your blessings.

—Irving Berlin

Lesson in the Park

You know how we girls have a habit of putting our entire lives in our purses? I am certainly no different. In my purse I had a little handy, keepsake knife/tool with my name engraved on it, given to me by Brenda Gunter. I also kept the normal things such as a checkbook, credit cards, and makeup for a touch-up . . . when my car was vandalized and my purse was stolen. The feeling was awful.

Often, I placed my purse in the backseat floor while I took my daily walk. Not only did the robbers take my cash and gift cards from Christmas and Summer's birthday, they also stole my purse Matthew and Jennifer had given me for Christmas. Everything was gone! Luckily, I had my keys and cell phone, so I immediately called my husband; he called the police, and they both met me at the park.

This was the first time I had ever felt like a victim. There was glass everywhere and I was a little distraught. But then I started to be grateful that, even though I was close by during the robbery, and like Matthew Henry, I was not harmed. God had shielded me and taught me a lesson I have not forgotten.

The Big Picture

Sometimes we have to pick ourselves up, forget the losses, knowing that *things* can be replaced. It doesn't take long to see the big picture. That's when we lift our hands in praise to God for His protecting power.

Many times it is a day-to-day survival. And that's all we need, one day's "manna." If we have the hope and faith needed for that day, then that gets us one day closer to a miracle or one day closer to heaven. Either way, we win.

Recently, I read this on Facebook: "Once the storm is over, you won't remember how you made it through or how you managed to survive. You won't even be sure, in fact, whether the storm is really over. But one thing is certain: When you come out of the storm, you won't be the same person who walked in." God's plan far exceeds our circumstances.

In the meantime, He is teaching us *patience*. We cannot see all the landmines out there that could potentially hinder our walk with God, but He does, and we must be patient and pay close attention to the Spirit's leading. When the impulse toward negative thinking looms, I like to create acrostics to help keep me positive and counting my blessings. Maybe the following acrostic about *patience* will help you, as it does me, to work through the things that keep me from being patient:

Pray and have a positive mind-set
Adjust my attitude
Thank God for all I have
Imitate Christ
Expect that all is well
Nix negative thoughts that are not God's plan

Care about those around me
Experience more of God's grace

Be patient and know that God is in control and that He holds the future in His hands.

Faith Builders

We've all been there . . . feeling like we are the only one who has ever suffered a loss. That's when we turn our focus again on what I call *faith builders*—those things that cause our faith to rise up. It may be a song, a book, a call from a friend who makes us laugh or cry, a church service, and especially God's Word. The Psalms are so heavily marked in my Bible because David and the other writers not only encouraged themselves in the Lord, but the words they wrote are straight from the heart of God. Who cannot be encouraged when reading this psalm: "For the Lord God is our sun and our shield. He gives us grace and glory. The Lord will withhold no good thing from those who do what is right. O Lord of Heaven's Armies, what joy for those who trust in you" (84:11-12 NLT).

Recently, a well-known pastor tragically lost his son and he said, "When the tide is out in your life, true friends rush in." This is so true. God has provided family and friends who rushed in just when we needed them.

Barbara Smith is a good friend I have had the opportunity to spend time with lately. We have a routine. Our time together starts with coffee and splitting a pastry. Next, we go next door to Firehouse Subs and split a sandwich and chips. Then we find our way to the next shop in the strip mall and get a frozen yogurt with all kinds of yummy toppings. It takes us about four hours to complete, but oh what fun we have. You know, there is another restaurant at the other end. Maybe next time we will start there and work our way in the opposite direction!

Encouragers

About eighteen months ago, I was visiting with a friend, Gail Spivey, who was the first one to mention that I needed to write a book to share Summer's story. In the few weeks that followed, I had three other individuals tell me the same thing. I'm amazed that at no time before or since then has anyone said that to me. It was surreal. Since my teenage years, we have so many wonderful memories of our times together. She's a friend who takes care of those she loves.

While ministering in different parts of the country, we basically saw each other at the General Assembly. So every two years, we would pick up where we left off. People close to me know I love my coffee, but when I drink so much, there is not much room left for water and other liquids that are necessary and so important for hydration. I can depend on Gail making sure I drink water. One time we had to buy a tote bag from the exhibits to carry our daily allotted amount. I was waterlogged at first. We all need people to care for us and, as the old love song says, "Little things mean a lot."

My husband's former assistant, Sandy Black, started mailing Summer the church bulletin when we lived in South Carolina because she knows she loves to receive mail. Even if we had gotten one the previous Sunday at church (which meant we got 10% off at Silver Bay!), she still mailed it. Pastor Black and Sandy moved to another church and we moved to Tennessee, but Summer still gets a church bulletin. Sandy receives nothing for this grateful gesture, except a thank-you every now and then—but what joy it brings Summer. If for some reason it's a day or so late, she asks, "Where is my mail?"

COUNTING MY BLESSINGS

Fun and Fellowship

In October 2009, I had the opportunity to attend the International Women's Conference in San Francisco, California. I love when I *have* to go to events of this nature. I always tell my husband, "You know, I *have* to go," which means he is left in charge of Summer. I don't get to arrive early for much shopping or stay later because of needing to get back home, but I take full advantage of the opportunity.

Becky Copley, Pam Childers, and I traveled together to this particular conference. We had such a great time. Even though we had responsibilities during the conference, I received so much from the speakers and being with my friends and sisters from across the country. It seemed we cried and emptied out our souls and refilled them with laughter. We had to take the *red-eye* flight coming home, and that within itself can explain the craziest of our behavior. The term *red-eye* derives from the symptoms of fatigue and having red eyes, which can be caused or aggravated by late-night travel. Our eyes were not aggravated at all by the flight. They may have been red, but it was from all the laughter. That was a trip I will never forget.

A SUMMER STORY
OF GOD'S ENDURING GRACE

Kathy Barger and I have been friends for a very long time. We met in Macon, Georgia, while attending the same church. We went to school, youth camp, camp meeting, Lee Day, took music lessons, and any and all events we could attend together. I will always remember our trip to the General Assembly in Dallas, Texas. We were just teenagers, but we found someone to ride with and had a blast.

Since we were inexperienced travelers, we got the shock of our lives when we looked at the check after ordering room service. It was only one sandwich for both of us, but quite expensive for two hitchhikers from Georgia. She always had my best interest at heart. You know the kind: when I ate six hot Krispy Kreme donuts that melt in your mouth, she made sure I exercised to make up for the extra junk food. She would put me out in a parking lot and drive slowly as I ran alongside the car to burn the calories I had consumed.

When my mother passed away, I will never forget that Kathy was the one who assisted me with Summer. She also helped me with the cleaning and sorting through all my mother's things. She and her husband, Steve, loaded my dad's boxes and moved him to his new home as well. We couldn't have done it with so much ease without them. I am forever grateful.

Summer's Home

One of my dreams is to have a place, or a home, bearing Summer's name for special-needs children who don't have anyone to care for them. Thanks to Cathy Gillum, there is still a "Summer's Room" at the state parsonage in South Carolina. One day, I'm believing there will be a "Summer's Home." *It could happen!*

Proverbs 16:24 says, "Pleasant words are like a honeycomb, sweetness to the soul and health to the bones" (NKJV). There are many, many that add sweetness to my soul, and I am better because of it. Only eternity will reveal the entire story.

CHAPTER TWELVE

You turned my wailing into dancing; you removed my sackcloth and clothed me with joy.

—Psalm 30:11

DANCING THROUGH THE PAIN

ONE OF MY FAVORITE BOOKS IS *DARING TO DANCE WITH God*, by Jeff Walling. Right up front, on the cover leaf, he describes what it is like to dance with God:

- Relaxing in His embrace and trusting His strong arms
- Releasing the power of the Spirit within you to give you joy beyond measure
- Reveling in the unexpected and celebrating the divine surprise that is new each day
- Rejoicing out loud at the grace and beauty God provides and ignoring the calls of the crowd to sit down and be silent

The image of dancing with our Maker may sound bizarre and maybe sacrilegious to Christians raised in a traditional church and lifestyle, but we could stop with the first bullet above and say, "That's exactly what I want to do: relax in His embrace, and trust His strong arms." Can we find a better lifestyle? I don't think so. However, many Christians are mired in so many "don'ts" that the idea of celebrating and dancing through the pain is completely foreign—if not sinful.

Music has played (no pun intended) a big part in the lives of the Propes family. God has blessed my husband and son with tremendous musical talent, and as a family, we hope we have given back to Him in ministry. Earlier in chapter 4, I quoted what Tommy had written on the cover of a record album we made early in our ministry while evangelizing. We love music and understand the importance it can play in an individual's life and worship service.

Growing up, my husband's favorite instrument was probably the drums, and, as a teenager, he traveled with a semiprofessional group doing just that. It also afforded him the opportunity to play with professional groups. Music was his first church job, unless you count helping his mother clean the church as a young boy. Before and while being a full-time student at Lee, he served as a minister of music. I worked at Lee full-time and attended school part-time.

We've often joked saying, "We can harmonize with anyone!" Music has not only fed our souls spiritually, but it also provided a place of service and ministry for us to make a living in those early years.

Thankfully, my son takes after his dad. He's naturally talented and has six guitars of various types—including a collectible 1969 Fender Jazz bass his dad gave him. I only wish I had practiced more during those piano lessons my parents provided for me—if I could only go back. However, since my husband could play, we were still seen as a good "package" for hire.

A 'Mini' Sermon

After returning home from a preaching assignment, my husband related the following phenomenal story to me, which I labeled as a *mini sermon,* because it relates to how we perceive the "storms" and the painful experiences in our lives:

> While flying into Hartford, Connecticut, I witnessed an unusual phenomenon of nature. As the plane began its descent, I happened to look out the window on the left side of the plane and noticed an extremely severe thunderstorm taking place. Then I looked to the right of the plane, and, much to my surprise, the sun was shining ever so brightly. All was calm and seemed beautifully at rest. Again, I looked back to the left and there was the storm—just as dark and unsettling as it was a moment

before. I looked back to the right of the plane, and the sun was shining just as brightly as it was a moment ago. *Amazing,* I thought! Obviously, it totally depended on which direction I chose to look as to what the forecast would be. I thought, *There is a sermon somewhere in this! In this walk of faith, life's journey, I can choose to look at the storms which will invariably come my way or I can choose to turn toward God, the author and finisher of my faith!* So the question is this: Which direction am I going to look?

Barriers to Dancing With God

Throughout Scripture, God's people have celebrated and danced with shouts of victory. When I search my on-line concordance in the NIV, I find the first mention of *celebrating* in Exodus 31:16: "The Israelites are to observe the Sabbath, celebrating it for the generations to come as a lasting covenant." Then in 1 Chronicles 13:8, we read, "David and all the Israelites were celebrating with all their might before God, with songs and with harps, lyres, tam-bourines, cymbals and trumpets" (see also 2 Sam. 6:5). And my favorite is Esther 8:17: "In every province and in every city, wherever the edict of the king went, there was joy and gladness among the Jews, with feasting and celebrating."

These are just a few examples in the Old Testament. If

we search for the word *rejoice*, we are given 133 scriptures that admonish us to be glad and rejoice! But . . . oh, those "buts" create intimidation and forbid us to step out on the dance floor. Breaking down those walls of fear, criticism, and resentment that keep us from dancing with God in celebration is not for the fainthearted. It's a shame, but these barriers can even become so comfortable (and self-righteous) that we use them as excuses to sit on the sidelines and refuse to open our hearts fully to God's grace and joy.

In the New Testament, Paul and Silas didn't wait until they experienced a breakthrough to praise and thank God. In the midst of difficult circumstances, they praised God and received the breakthrough they desired:

> Around midnight Paul and Silas were praying and singing hymns to God, and the other prisoners were listening. Suddenly, there was a massive earthquake, and the prison was shaken to its foundations. All the doors immediately flew open, and the chains of every prisoner fell off! (Acts 16:25-26 NLT).

Paul and Silas praised God even when their backs were bleeding and their feet and hands were in chains. Despite the pain and suffering they were enduring, they praised God anyway; as a result, God shook the very foundations of the prison, setting them free.

David disrobed himself of his royalty, dignity, and inhibitions as he danced before and worshiped the Lord. The Scripture implies that David danced with all his might. In other words, David put his entire mind, soul, and body into reverent worship to God who is so worthy of all praise.

Letting God Lead

We must be willing to trust that God will give guidance to our lives. And we have to be willing to let God lead; we must follow.

If you look at the word *guidance* closely, you will see the word *dance* at the end. We've all seen, read about, or even participated in a slow dance, and we know the concept of how it works: one person leads and the other follows. When two people try to lead, nothing feels right. The movement doesn't flow with the music, and everything is quite uncomfortable and jerky. However, when one person relaxes and allows the other to lead, both bodies begin to flow with the music.

The one leading gives gentle cues, perhaps with a nudge to the back or by pressing lightly in one direction or another. When only one leads, it's as if two become one body, moving beautifully together. The dance takes surrender, willingness, and attentiveness from one person, and gentle guidance and skill from the other.

The word *guidance* begins with the letter *g*, which could stand for God. The *g* is followed by the letters *u* and *i*: *God, u, i, dance* (God, you, and I dance!). I want God to guide my life—I need Him to guide my life. I want to do as David did when he danced unashamedly before the Lord with all his heart.

I love the worship chorus based on John 8:36, where Jesus declares, "So if the Son sets you free, you will be free indeed." The Newsboys sing this in a contemporary worship chorus that repeats this truth: "I am free to run . . . to dance . . . to live for Christ."

Dancing the Tough Tunes

We don't always feel the joy of the Lord. I didn't feel it when Summer suffered the stroke. But I knew I needed to somehow reach deep into my soul and muster up enough faith to reach up to Him. I found a handicapped-accessible bathroom that was large enough for me to walk back and forth. It was just me and God, and I would sing, "Jehovah

Jireh, my provider, You are more than enough for me." It worked. In a few moments, I could feel my spirit rising.

My family is not the only Christian family who has suffered through tough times. Ironically, these times of heartbreak bring out the best in our prayer life. Whatever the crisis—a financial setback, a medical emergency, a wayward child, the loss of a loved one, a major disappointment, or any other catastrophe—will crank up our communication with God.

One of my friends, Jan Timmerman, expressed it this way: "Everything God allows to touch my life has already passed through His hands. Everything has a purpose that will ultimately take me to my destiny. This process positions me to receive a special grace from God that I could not have received any other way. I am aware of the Enemy's strategy to keep God's will from becoming a reality in my life as it relates to my purpose. The adversary knows, if he can keep me focused on what is wrong, I will avoid doing what is right by placing my total trust in God. In reality, it is the power of vision. We cannot look at where we have been; we must look at where we are going."

Fancy dance steps, or experience with simple steps, are not prerequisites for celebrating God's blessings. Taking part in the dance doesn't promise an instant solution but, rather, the possibility of an eventual one.

When Jesus was teaching the Pharisees and the experts in the Law, He said:

"To what can I compare this generation? They are like children sitting in the marketplaces and calling out to others: 'We played the flute for you, and you did not dance; we sang a dirge, and you did not mourn'" (Matt. 11:16-17).

There is something fundamentally wrong with a faith that is never expressed in some way. Though the style may vary, physical expressions of faith and joy in Christ are part of the fabric of Pentecostal worship. Any Christian who never cries about the sacrifice of the Savior or expresses with exuberance the thankfulness for the gift of salvation is missing out. Could it be that we are so concerned and worried about praising God in the right way, at the right time, that we end up not praising Him at all?

Regardless of our circumstances, Christ calls us to praise Him with abandon. David declared:

I will praise you, O Lord, with all my heart; I will tell of all your wonders. I will be glad and rejoice in you; I will sing praise to your name, O Most High (Ps. 9:1-2).

What happens if we bottle up our passion and refuse to dance, thinking, *Let's not go overboard with this celebrating!* That's when we not only lose our joy, but we may also begin to question others' motives.

When the ark of the covenant was brought back to Jerusalem, David stopped the parade and made an offering, thanking God for returning His favor to them. Then, without his kingly robe and crown, David "danced with all his might before the Lord" (see 2 Sam. 6:14). Overjoyed, he invited others to join him in the celebration. Praise and pure adoration to God for His goodness and mercy will attract others to join the celebration.

The Dance of the Ages

The dance I've discussed in this chapter is an unending one that is exuberant in times of good news, and mild in moments of gradual healing. However, it will never come to a complete end until we join Him around the throne in the celestial ballroom that is big enough for all the saints to join in and celebrate throughout the ages!

Summer, I'm so glad that on your good days you can turn the music up and start tapping your toes to the beat. I believe your future is locked up so tightly within the promises of God that no stroke or seizure can stop the dance.

My sweet Summer, this is your story. I still hope for you and, like the words of Lee Ann Womack's song says, "If you get the choice to sit it out or dance, I hope you dance!" And I, along with many, many other family members and friends, will join you in the dance!

SUMMER WITH JAN AND LARRY TIMMERMAN

AFTERWORD

You came near when I called you, and
you said, "Do not fear."

—Lamentations 3:57

Seldom do we have a better opportunity to experience Christ personally than those times when we face a terrifying crisis, such as the Memorial Day weekend I have talked about in this book. In the middle of the disaster of helping to save my child's life, I experienced His grace, power, wisdom, and sustaining presence. This book is a testimony of how God has guided my steps, directed my life, and taught me to rely fully on Him.

Interwoven into Summer's story are numerous stories of individuals who have touched my life in a powerful way. It would be impossible to mention everyone who ministered to me and my family; but it is amazing what a note, a listening ear, a season of prayer, a hug (with no lecture about the sovereignty of God), a meal, or some free baby-sitting with a sick child can mean. I am so grateful for the individuals who have gone beyond the call of duty and became "agents of compassion" in my life.

As God weaves His pattern into the fabric of our lives, sometimes we are forced to sit in a darkened room where we are unable to understand what He is doing and can't comprehend any possible good in the darkness. Yet, if we fix our focus on our faithful Weaver, He has promised we will know later that the most exquisite work of our life was done during those days of darkness. As I look back over my life, my deepest intimacy with Him has come from the dark times. The lessons I learned when the black clouds hovered are lessons of faith, perseverance, and trust—reassuring me that my wise, loving Lord not only walks with me, but He leads me every step of the way.

Effective living begins with a choice to follow Christ, and continues as an uncompromised and nonnegotiable commitment to becoming fully devoted to Christ. I am reminded that when Christ recruited His disciples, He was upfront about the issue. He did not sugarcoat the cost of following Him, neither did He dupe them into following. "Follow Me" was the first and last thing Christ said to Peter. It is for us as well.

Just in case you think God has not done anything for you lately, remember how active He is every day, keeping out anything that would be more than you could bear (see

1 Cor. 10:13) and prohibiting anything that He cannot turn to glory and gain (see Rom. 8:28; James 1:2-5). Every night when we place our heads on the pillow, we can express our gratitude for the fact that Christ and His angels have been busy on our behalf, guarding and guiding us all the day, and guaranteeing that we cannot be fatally damaged by an adversary who seeks to destroy us.

The challenge for us who strive to be devoted followers of Christ is that our commitment must express itself with increasing measures of consistency in a world that trumpets the importance of charting our own course. We cannot become self-led. We who have embraced Christ as redeemer and friend need to do more than call Him *Lord*. We must embrace Him as the supreme leader of our lives. We must reject the strong impulse to control our lives (see Prov. 3:5-6).

I believe our greatest challenge, however, is the ability to transfer personal authority to Him. Even though we call Him *Christ* and refer to Him as *Lord*, few of us want Him to be the leader unconditionally. We live with the sense that we can do a pretty good job of managing our own lives. I know of people who will listen to His advice and keep Him on hand in case of an emergency, but to transfer full authority to Him is less than appealing to them. Their destinies are crafted on the drawing board of their own wants and desires.

Recently, I watched a television remake of the film *Sabrina*, in which Harrison Ford plays a second generation CEO who is savagely addicted to gaining his inheritance. When he meets the daughter of his family's chauffeur, he is intrigued by her qualities. As the lives of a commoner and a conqueror merge, he follows her to Paris. Drained and ready for more to life, he says brokenly, "I've been following in footsteps all my life. Help me, Sabrina fair. You're the only one who can save me."

This moving moment in the movie is a metaphor of our relationship to Christ, our Creator. Many are tired and disillusioned, achieving success without significance. Addicted to what they thought were objects of liberation, and weary of working for an end that only leads to emptiness, they look into the face of Christ, who has promised abundant life. In a wonderful moment of surrender, I invite anyone reading this book who experiences these feelings of failure and insignificance to pray this simple prayer: *Help me, Father. You are the only One who can save me.*

And Christ replies with two simple words: "Follow Me." Only then can we begin life's ultimate adventure.

> So then, just as you received Christ Jesus as Lord, continue to live in him, rooted and built up in him, strengthened in the faith as you were taught, and overflowing with thankfulness (Col. 2:6-7).

pure life
photography by Tammy Rockwell

INDEX OF MEDICAL TERMS

Angiogram is an X-ray test that uses a special dye and camera (fluoroscopy) to take pictures of the blood flow in an artery (such as the aorta) or a vein (such as the vena cava).

Anticonvulsant drugs typically are used to control seizures in people who have epilepsy.

Antiepileptic medications (AEDs) are used to treat seizures. There is no formula to choose which seizure medicine to use for a particular patient. No single medicine dominates for effectiveness, and all have various side effects. Doctors and patients choose AEDs after considering which side effects should be avoided in particular cases, convenience of use, cost, and physician experience.

Arteriovenous Malformations (AVMs) are abnormal connections between arteries and veins.

Behavioral Neurology & Neuropsychiatry is defined as a medical subspecialty committed to better understanding links between neuroscience and behavior, and to the care of individuals with neurologically based behavioral disturbances.

Brain hemorrhage is a type of stroke, caused by an artery in the brain bursting and causing localized bleeding in the surrounding tissues. This bleeding kills brain cells.

Catamenial seizure is a type of seizure that is associated with the female menstrual cycle due to fluctuations in hormone levels.

Cerebral hemorrhage is uncontrolled bleeding in the brain. It is always an emergency. Seek immediate medical care (call 911) for serious symptoms, such as severe headache, nausea, numbness or weakness, loss of the ability to see or speak, seizures, or change in level of consciousness or alertness, such as passing out or unresponsiveness.

Cerebrum (or cortex) is the largest part of the human brain.

Computed Tomography (CT) scan is an imaging method that uses x-rays to create pictures of cross-sections of the body.

Craniotomy is surgical removal of part of the skull to expose the brain.

Diastat is a gel preparation of *diazepam* (tranquilizer / muscle relaxant) for rectal administration in the treatment of cluster seizures or prolonged seizures in the patient who has refractory epilepsy.

INDEX OF MEDICAL TERMS

EEG Video Monitoring allows prolonged simultaneous recording of the patient's behavior and the EEG. Seeing EEG and video data at the same time permits precise correlation between seizure activity in the brain and the patient's behavior during seizures.

Electrocardiogram (EKG or ECG) is a test that checks for problems with the electrical activity of your heart.

Electroencephalography (EEG) is a test to measure electrical activity of the brain.

Emergency Medical Service (EMS) is a service providing out-of-hospital acute care and transport.

Emergency Medical Technician (EMT) is one who responds to emergency calls, performs certain medical procedures, and transports patients to hospital in accordance with protocols and guidelines established by physician medical directors.

Emergency Number 911 allows a caller to contact local emergency services for assistance.

Emergency Room (ER) is a medical treatment facility specializing in acute care of patients who are present without prior appointment, either by their own means or by ambulance.

Failure to thrive refers to children whose current weight, or rate of weight gain, is significantly lower than that of other children of similar age and gender.

Fontanel is a soft membranous spot on the head of an infant due to incomplete fusion of the cranial bones.

Grand mal is a severe epilepsy characterized by seizures which are initially tonic and then become clonic and by loss of consciousness.

Hemorrhagic stroke occurs when a weakened blood vessel ruptures. Two types of weakened blood vessels usually cause hemorrhagic stroke: *aneurysms* and *arteriovenous malformations* (AVMs).

Hippocampus is part of the temporal lobe and emotion system of the brain (the *limbic system*) and is in charge of transferring information into memory.

Hydrocephalus is the buildup of fluid in the cavities (ventricles) deep within the brain. The excess fluid increases the size of the ventricles and puts pressure on the brain.

INDEX OF MEDICAL TERMS

Intensive Care Unit (ICU)—also known as a **Critical Care Unit (CCU), Intensive Therapy Unit or Intensive Treatment Unit (ITU)**—is a special department of a hospital or health-care facility that provides to patients with the most severe and life-threatening illnesses and injuries, and who require constant, close monitoring, and support from specialist equipment and medication in order to maintain normal bodily functions. They are staffed by highly trained doctors and critical-care nurses who specialize in caring for seriously ill patients.

Magnetic Resonance Imaging (MRI) scan is an imaging test that uses powerful magnets and radio waves to create pictures of the body. It does not use radiation (x-rays).

Medically Induced Coma is when a patient receives a controlled dose of an anesthetic, to cause a temporary coma or a deep state of unconsciousness. This type of coma is used to protect the brain from swelling by reducing the metabolic rate of brain tissue, as well as the cerebral blood flow. Throughout a medically induced coma, a patient's critical life functions are constantly monitored by an anesthesiologist or other physician in a critical-care setting only.

Mitral Valve Prolapse (MVP). The mitral valve controls blood flow on the left side of the heart. The valve opens and closes with each heartbeat. It works like a one-way gate, letting blood flow from the upper-heart chamber to the lower chamber. When you have *mitral valve prolapse*, the valve closes after blood flows through, but the valve bulges backward a little. It looks like a tiny parachute or balloon as it bulges.

Neonatal Intensive Care Unit (NICU) is an intensive care unit specializing in the care of ill or premature newborn infants.

Neurologist is a doctor who specializes in neurology. The neurologist treats disorders that affect the brain, spinal cord, and nerves.

Neurology is the branch of medicine concerned with the study and treatment of disorders of the nervous system. The nervous system is a complex, sophisticated system that regulates and coordinates body activities. It has two major divisions: the *central nervous system*—the brain and spinal cord; and the *peripheral nervous system*—all other neural elements, such as eyes, ears, skin, and other "sensory receptors.

Neurosurgeon is someone who does surgery on the nervous system (especially the brain).

INDEX OF MEDICAL TERMS

Neurosurgery is surgery on any part of the nervous system.

Occupational Therapy (OT) is the use of treatments to develop, recover, or maintain the daily living and work skills of patients with a physical, mental, or developmental condition.

Paramedic is a health-care professional who works in emergency medical situations.

Physical Therapy (PT) is primarily concerned with the remediation of impairments and disabilities and the promotion of mobility, functional ability, quality of life, and movement potential—through examination, evaluation, diagnosis, and physical intervention carried out by physical therapists.

Positron Emission Tomography (PET) scan is an imaging test that uses a radioactive substance called a *tracer* to look for disease in the body.

Postictal period represents the end of a seizure and the transition back to the individual's normal state.

Prophylactic Antibiotic Therapy is a treatment with antibiotics, beginning just before a surgical procedure, to minimize or prevent development of infection.

Seizures are uncontrolled electrical activity in the brain that may lead to symptoms that may range from mild loss of attention to violent muscular contractions that can lead to death. There are two types of seizures:

- **Generalized seizures** involve both sides of the brain from the start of the attack. Common subtypes include **tonic-clonic (grand mal)** and **absence seizures (petit mal)**. Febrile and infantile spasms are two types of generalized seizures that occur almost exclusively in young children.

- **Partial (or focal) seizures** are the second major seizure type. These begin in a specific area of the brain and may be contained there. Or they may spread to the entire brain. With **simple partial seizures**, the person remains conscious; **complex partial seizures** involve impaired consciousness.

Speech Therapy specializes in communication disorders as well as swallowing disorders.

Spinal Tap (lumbar puncture) is a procedure to collect and look at the fluid (cerebrospinal fluid, or CSF) surrounding the brain and spinal cord.

Status epilepticus is a series of seizures or one prolonged seizure, usually a grand mal type. It can be life-threatening due to lack of oxygen. It is a medical emergency.

Stroke or Cerebrovascular Accident (CVA) is the rapid loss of brain function due to disturbance in the blood supply to the brain. This can be due to ischemia (lack of blood flow) caused by blockage (thrombosis, arterial embolism), or a hemorrhage.

Subacute Bacterial Endocarditis (SBE) is a chronic bacterial infection of the valves of the heart.

Temporal Lobes (located just above the ears) are one of the four main lobes or regions of the cerebral cortex. Structures of the limbic system—including the olfactory cortex, amygdala, and the hippocampus—are located within the temporal lobes. The temporal lobes play an important role in organizing sensory input, auditory perception, language and speech production, as well as memory association and formation.

Temporal Lobe Seizures are seizures that originate in the two temporal lobes of the brain. The temporal lobes process emotions, fight-or-flight reactions, and are important for short-term memory. Some symptoms of a temporal lobe seizure may be related to these functions, including having odd feelings—such as euphoria, fear, panic, and déjà-vu.

Vagus Nerve Stimulator (VNS) is similar to a pacemaker, surgically implanted under the skin, usually on the chest, which provides short bursts of electrical energy directed into the brain via the vagus nerve, a large nerve in the neck.

Ventilator is a machine that supports breathing.

WADA Test is used to determine which side of the brain controls language function and also how important each side of the brain is in regard to memory function.

X-rays are a type of electromagnetic radiation, just like visible light.